DATE DUE

organic, shaken and stirred

organic, shaken and stirred

hip highballs, modern martinis, and other totally green cocktails

PAUL ABERCROMBIE

The Harvard Common Press
Boston, Massachusetts

The Harvard Common Press
535 Albany Street
Boston, Massachusetts 02118
www.harvardcommonpress.com

Printed in China
Printed on recycled, acid-free paper

Library of Congress Cataloging-in-Publication Data
Abercrombie, Paul.
  Organic, shaken and stirred : hip highballs, modern martinis, and other
totally green cocktails / Paul Abercrombie.
     p. cm.
  Includes index.
  ISBN 978-1-55832-436-7
 1. Cocktails. 2. Natural foods. I. Title.
  TX951.A28 2009
  641.8'74--dc22

                            2008055568

Special bulk-order discounts are available on this and other Harvard
Common Press books. Companies and organizations may purchase books
for premiums or resale, or may arrange a custom edition, by contacting
the Marketing Director at the address above.

Book design by Elizabeth Van Itallie
Photography by Jerry Errico
Drink styling by Helen Jones
Prop styling by Kristi Schiffman

10 9 8 7 6 5 4 3 2 1

for gail

acknowledgments

Thanks above all to my wife, Gail, for more than I can ever fit or express here (and sorry about the kitchen now looking like a bar), and to my son, Ewan, for sometimes letting Daddy play dinosaurs with a cocktail shaker in one hand.

So many people helped me with this book, graciously opening their Rolodexes and recipe boxes, including Allison Evanow, Neal Fraser, H. Joseph Ehrmann, Enrico Caruso, Paul Davis, Todd Thrasher, Lance Hanson, Matt Baris, Lance Mayhew, Natalie Bovis-Nelsen, Phoenix Kelly-Rappa, Scott Beattie, Gray Ottley, Kate LaCroix, Alberta Straub, Melanie and Lizzie Asher, Lisa Averbuch, Sabrina Moreno-Dolan, Vanessa Polk, Melkon Khosrovian, Litty Mathew, Ann Tuennerman, Tonia Guffey, Gina Chersevani, Bryant Terry, Gianpiero Ruggeri, Chris Cason, Mike Sherwood, Debbie Rizzo, Willy Shine, Dori Bryant, Gianfranco Verga, my brother-in-law Snow Martin and his friends (for their valiant service, along with my neighbors, as drink testers), my "research" assistant John Fowler, Bill Frederick, and all the folks whose recipes appear in these pages; please check out the credits on pages 168–171 for their names and creations. Thank you to all of you.

Thanks also to Danielle Egan-Miller for finding a home for this book at The Harvard Common Press, and to my editor, Pam Hoenig, who is more talented and patient than I deserve. I'm also grateful to copyeditor Christine Corcoran Cox, without whose help these words would scarcely be recognizable as English.

I'm sure I've forgotten to thank many others. I'd blame cocktails, but the fault is all mine. I owe you a drink.

contents

introduction

Forget painting the town red: Today's smart set is painting the town green. As in organic-cocktail green.

The hottest trend in the bar scene these days is eco-chic cocktails. We're not talking froufrou frappés or the tippler's equivalent of tofu. These are real drinks. Cutting-edge restaurants and bars are concocting healthful libations with fresh produce and unadulterated alcohol. Organic distilleries are popping up. Even prefab cocktail mixers, once the tint and taste of nothing found in nature, are going organic.

People are pouring organic cocktails for many of the same reasons they're choosing organic food—to avoid artificial ingredients, including synthetic pesticides, that are harmful to their bodies as well as to the land and ecosystems, and to help support sustainable farming and environmentally friendly packaging. (Think of it as giving new meaning to the phrase "drinking responsibly.")

The growing awareness of organic foods' benefits to our bodies and our planet is finding expression in a culinary approach to cocktails. "The kitchen is heading to the bar," says Natalie Bovis-Nelsen, who teaches The Liquid Muse Sustainable Sips eco-friendly cocktail classes around the nation. "Mixologists, bartenders, and even home cocktailians are discovering that organic ingredients, from fresh fruits to herbs, also make killer cocktails."

Or as Gina Chersevani, bartender at the Washington, D.C., restaurant PS 7's, puts it: "You don't have to sacrifice taste and health just because you're going out nightclubbing." What's more, medical experts say that organic alcohol is lower in methanol—the toxin responsible for hangovers—than the nonorganic variety, which may mean one less reason to regret last night's revelry.

Walk into any halfway hip restaurant or bar, and you'll see that Gina is but one member of a growing movement that is shaking up the world of spirits. Few are as inspired in bringing natural ingredients to the bar as H. Joseph Ehrmann. He's so committed to preparing perfectly organic cocktails that his San Francisco saloon Elixir is officially recognized as one of the city's first green businesses. And if there is such a thing as a healthy cocktail, Trudy Thomas is making them. At the Camelback Inn resort and spa in Scottsdale, Arizona, where she is beverage director, Trudy is working her own artisanal alchemy with original concoctions such as her Detox Margarita and other spa-inspired delicacies fashioned from all manner of seasonal organic fruit and herb purees.

The recipes in *Organic, Shaken and Stirred* will let you join the fun. The book is a concise yet power-packed organic cocktail how-to, offering everything from tips on where and how to score the best organic herbs, fruits, veggies, and liquors around town—and the planet—to goof-proof instructions for assembling dozens of updated classics and wildly inventive new creations from the food world's superstar mixologists. I've consulted today's best and brightest creators of organic cocktails, and in these pages you'll find dozens of their most popular drinks, plus some of my own variations. Come to think of it, you can be served many of these drinks by their creators, whose bars and restaurants are listed in the Drink Credits section beginning on page 168. Finding the right recipe for any mood or occasion is as easy as heading to one of the book's four chapters organized by flavor—Clean and Classic, Lush and Fruity, Fresh and Zesty, and From the Garden—or to the Punch and Pitcher chapter, which features drinks that are perfect to enjoy with friends.

Organic, Shaken and Stirred will guide you as you shop, shake, and sip your way to a whole new manner of enjoying what's in your cocktail glass. I'll help you brush up on key mixology skills, get a grip on what bar gear you do (and don't) need, and learn to make the organic cocktail world's most mouthwatering libations.

Let's raise the bar and toast to a fresh new take on the cocktail tradition.

everything you need to know to build a green bar

stocking the green bar

Whether you are a professional bartender or the proud owner of a couple of highball glasses left over from college, there is one simple rule for stocking your organic cocktail bar: No drink ever rises above the quality of its ingredients.

The advantages of avoiding pesticides, fertilizers, or fungicides in your alcohol are manifold. Spirits are distilled, and some distillers believe that organically grown grains, sugarcane, and potatoes have better cell structure than their nonorganic counterparts and that their natural microorganisms encourage the process of fermentation. According to many distillers, allowing natural microorganisms (rather than various so-called enhancers, or enzymes, that speed up and intensify the fermentation process) to encourage fermentation results in a cleaner, purer product and better-tasting spirits.

What's more, organic growing methods are healthier for growers, more sustainable, and kinder to the land and water, and result in food that often plain tastes better—a lot better.

Distilleries and others in the cocktail-industrial complex are paying attention to the organic trend. Since organic-spirits pioneer Allison Evanow launched Square One Organic Spirits with vodka made from 100 percent organic American rye several years ago, she has been joined almost monthly by new commercial producers of organic liquors. Even mixers are getting the organic treatment.

Anybody who goes to the trouble of making a certified organic spirit will tout this designation—adorning bottle labels with the word "organic" and proudly displaying official credentials such as the USDA Organic logo. Yet many spirits unable to earn the right to be labeled organic are made with organic ingredients and can be found easily through an Internet search. Better yet, drop by your neighborhood liquor store and seek out the help of the more seasoned employees or managers. Shops that carry fine wines or have staffers with job titles like "senior beverage consultant" or "sommelier" are most likely to offer guidance in finding good organic cocktail ingredients.

What follows is an overview of what's going on in ecologically friendly imbibing. Please check the Online Resources section (page 171) for the websites of the companies discussed if you'd like more information.

organic (and almost organic) vodka

Square One Organic Spirits released its first vodka in 2006, making this northern California company a relative old hand at turning out organic spirits. Like many start-ups in the spirits world, Square One does no distilling. Rather, it contracts with an Idaho distillery that uses 100 percent organically grown rye from North Dakota and water from Wyoming's Teton Mountain Range to create certified organic vodka. The result is among the very best organic vodkas. Super supple and clean, with earthy hints of rye, Square One's vodka has a versatility that makes it great in any cocktail—including martinis, which are unforgiving of lesser spirits. Square One vodka is also fine for sipping straight. Square One, headed by Allison Evanow, was among the first to introduce cucumber-flavored vodka; also rye-based, Square One Cucumber has excellent flavor and is (so far) the best in breed.

Square One also aims to be environmentally responsible. Byproducts from the fermentation of the rye used in its products become feed at nearby cattle farms. The company's bottle labels are made using bamboo pulp, sugarcane, cotton, and soy-based inks. And Square One is exploring the use of recycled glass for its bottles.

California's Napa Valley is home to hundreds of wineries, including the family-owned Charbay Winery & Distillery, which produces spirits of amazing quality and variety. Most of its vodkas aren't certified organic, though they are made with all-natural ingredients and are of very high quality. Organic fruits are used to make the distillery's excellent blood orange–, pomegranate–, and Meyer lemon–flavored vodkas.

Organic corn grown by a co-op of some 900 Minnesota farmers is transformed by Minneapolis's Phillips Distilling Company into velvety smooth Prairie Organic Vodka. Leftover corncobs and other biomass get recycled as fuel to power the stills.

Also from Minnesota is Crop Harvest Earth Company's trio of organic corn vodkas in straight, tomato, and cucumber flavors. All are excellent—especially the tomato version.

Certified organic and made from American grain, Vodka 14 is, like Square One, distilled in Idaho. But in blending and packaging its product, Vodka 14's maker, Altitude Spirits, goes the proverbial extra mile, opting for more ecologically friendly baked-on ink labels. Bottles are sealed with recyclable synthetic cork closures. Vodka 14 is sold in Colorado and parts of Tennessee, and can also be purchased online.

Launched several years ago in the California kitchen of Melkon Khosrovian and his wife, Litty Mathew, Modern Spirits sells a handful of organic spirits under the TRU label. The company's trio of certified organic vodkas made from American wheat includes straight, lemon, and vanilla flavors (the company also produces an organic gin). Modern Spirits is meticulous in its techniques, such as hand zesting organic California lemons and hand scraping organic bourbon vanilla beans. The results are very fine and smooth vodkas. What's more, TRU's green credentials include using soy-based inks and tree-free paper for labels, and recycled, recyclable, or biodegradable packaging. Plus, the company pledges to plant a tree for every bottle sold.

360 Vodka is good stuff, but it is not organic. However, Missouri-based maker McCormick Distilling is powered by renewable energy and uses environmentally friendly packaging, including bottles made from mostly recycled glass. For every one of the company's swing-top bottle closures you return in a prepaid envelope, the company donates a dollar to environmental groups.

Vermont's Green Mountain Distillers produces Sunshine Vodka, made from organic American corn. However, the product has limited distribution, so look for it online.

Even Anheuser-Busch, maker of Budweiser, is getting into the green-spirits game with its Purus brand of organic vodka, which is made in northern Italy from locally harvested organic wheat and alpine water. The labels are made using tree-free paper and soy-based inks.

Spunky Oregon micro-distillery Cascade Peak Spirits joins Square One as a woman-led company producing great vodka made from organic rye. Cascade Peak president and CEO Diane Paulson recently added a gin to the Organic Nation, or O-N, brand, and plans to introduce infused spirits and whiskey. Organic Nation spirits are available at select retailers around the country and online.

Colorado distillery Peak Spirits produces an ambitious—and delicious—array of organic spirits using fruit from its own organic orchards, including CapRock Organic Vodka. Made from organic grapes and mountain spring water, this certified organic vodka has a very nice round, clean taste. As of this writing, it is available only in Colorado, Nevada, and New Mexico.

Orange V Vodka is made using 100 percent organic grains, though the citrus juices used to infuse it are not organic. This is one nicely balanced infusion, nonetheless.

Like its name suggests, Utkins UK5 Organic Vodka comes from Britain. Made by Organic Spirits Company with organic rye from Germany, UK5 is credited with being the first certified organic vodka in the world. It's also the only unfiltered vodka, which would matter if there were any impurities to filter out. As it turns out, this is a very clean and smooth-tasting vodka.

Made in Kentucky from organic white corn grown in Illinois, Rain Organics Vodka is very light and mixes well with other ingredients. In addition to a straight vodka, the company also produces certified organic vodkas featuring new flavor combinations, including Cucumber Lime, Honey Mango Melon, Red Grape Hibiscus, and Lavender Lemonade.

The Norway-based vodka producer Christiania, which touts its product as "the world's smoothest vodka," gets its name from Norwegian King Christian IV, who in 1602 commissioned the recipe for this spirit. Made from organic Trondelag potatoes, this vodka has a faintly sweet quality.

While not technically organic, Hangar One Vodka is handmade with such love and fresh, high-quality ingredients (nothing artificial, no additives) that it deserves to be listed here. Distilled from pricey Viognier wine and blended with wheat vodka, Hangar One Vodka is wonderfully clean and pure. Craft Distillers, which makes Hangar One, also produces delicious fruit-infused vodkas, including Citron Buddha's Hand, Fraser River Raspberry, Kaffir Lime, and Mandarin Blossom versions.

And from Iceland, the land that gave the world Björk, comes Reyka, a wheat and barley grain vodka that, although not certified organic, may owe much of its super-clean taste to the ecologically conscious way it's produced. The company uses geothermal steam to power its distillery and indigenous lava rock to filter the spirit (most vodka is filtered through manmade charcoal).

organic gin

Gin has come a long way from the bathtub and kitchen sink, where Prohibition-era partyers used to cook up batches of it. Inspired by gin's recent renaissance, craft distillers are creating organic gins of high quality and distinct style.

Gin is basically vodka distilled with botanicals. The quality and quantity of botanicals used is crucial to a gin's taste. Construction begins with juniper berries, though any number of other herbs and roots can be included, depending on the taste you're going for.

The production of organic gins is, thankfully, catching up to that of vodka. Among the better brands is Juniper Green Organic Gin, fittingly distilled in central London, the town that made gin infamous in the mid eighteenth century, when gin consumption was rampant and its effects so destructive that gin was nicknamed "mother's ruin." Made with a riot of organic juniper berries, coriander, angelica root, and savory, Juniper Green is a very flavorful gin, but it won't overpower other ingredients in a cocktail.

Philadelphia Distilling, a craft producer of gin in Pennsylvania, is making Bluecoat American Dry Gin, an American-style (read: cleaner) gin made with organic juniper berries, which give it a nice spicy earthiness, along with angelica root and citrus peel. It's currently available in a number of states and online.

Colorado-based Peak Spirits produces a wonderfully balanced and flavorful spirit, CapRock Organic Dry Gin, made with a blend of high-desert fruits, blossoms, and spices, which are infused in an organic apple distillate. At this time, it is available only at retailers and restaurants in Colorado, Nevada, and New Mexico.

Cascade Peak Spirits' Organic Nation, or O-N, brand gin has a gentle herbaceous quality that makes for a versatile mixer. Organic Nation spirits currently are available only in Oregon.

organic rum

Distilled from fermented sugarcane juice or molasses, rum is one of the most versatile cocktail spirits. Organic versions are just now catching up to the demand. Among the first and best are Papagayo Organic White Rum, Papagayo Organic Fair Trade Golden Rum, and Papagayo Organic Spiced Rum. Made in Paraguay from sugarcane grown on small family farms, these award-winning rums can be tricky to find in the U.S., but the White and Spiced versions are imported here by Maison Jomere. Another organic option is Utkins Fair Trade White Rum, produced by Paraguayan farmers who are guaranteed a fair trade price for their produce.

Distilled from organic sugarcane juice, Rhum Clément Première Canne Premium Rum from Martinique is a wonderfully fruity white rum. Waste cane gets reused as fuel to power the distillery.

A close cousin to rum is cachaça (pronounced ka-SHAH-sa), Brazil's biggest cultural export since the samba and the key ingredient in its national drink, the Caipirinha. Unlike rum, which is made from fermented sugarcane juice and then aged in oak barrels, cachaça is made from fresh sugarcane juice.

Though not yet certified organic, Cuca Fresca's cachaças are distilled slowly and in small batches from organically grown and hand-cut Brazilian sugarcane. Cuca Fresca's premium silver cachaça tastes very fresh and bright. Its

Pura Gold gets its honey hues and mellow smoothness from more than three years of aging in oak barrels. Cuca Fresca's interest in environmental responsibility includes fundraising and donating a portion of the company's proceeds to rain forest conservation efforts.

organic tequila

Tequila is already one of the most natural of spirits. To be called tequila, it must be made entirely from natural blue agave plants grown and harvested only in the Mexican states of Guanjuato, Michoacan, Jalisco, Mayarit, or Tamaulipas. The world's first—and so far only—USDA-certified organic tequila, 4 Copas, goes further, eschewing all pesticides and using only organic yeast to kick-start fermentation. Waste is composted and used as fertilizer for the company's agave plants. The methane gas created during production is captured and used to fire 4 Copas's distillery steam engines. The company makes four kinds of tequila—blanco, reposado, añejo, and extra-añejo—all of which are excellent. Blanco, or "white," tequila is bottled immediately after being distilled; reposado, or "rested," tequila has remained in wood casks for a period of more than two months but no longer than twelve; añejo, meaning "vintage," refers to bottles aged for a minimum of one year; and extra-añejo, or "ultra-aged," has been aged for at least three years. In addition, 4 Copas produces special-release tequilas, including an añejo in a bottle festooned with a sea turtle, with all proceeds donated to sea turtle conservation.

bourbon, rye, and scotch

Only a few organic whiskeys exist, but some are more ecologically friendly—and tastier—than others. Whiskeys include any distilled spirit that's made from grain and aged until it develops the particular taste commonly associated with whiskey. Those most commonly used as cocktail ingredients are the American spirits bourbon and rye whiskey. Bourbons are made mostly of corn; ryes must be made from at least 51 percent rye grain.

For bourbon, I recommend Maker's Mark. It may not be organic, and it is a behemoth brand, but it could teach craft brewers a thing or two about being earth friendly. In fact, the company is a leader in sustainable distilling, with a distillery set on a state-certified nature preserve and a state-of-the-art recycling and wastewater treatment facility. Maker's Mark recently began using anaerobic digestion, a process that turns waste into bio-gas that is then used as a source of energy, offsetting up to 30 percent of the distillery's natural gas use. And, most importantly, Maker's Mark turns out some very fine bourbon.

Ecologically minded choices are fewer for rye whiskey. For taste, I prefer Russell's Reserve Rye, which, while not organic, is wonderfully spicy and lively and is also widely available.

Scotch whisky ("whisky" is spelled without the "e" if it comes from Scotland) tends to have an assertive personality that doesn't always mix well in cocktails. Still, I'd like to say hic-hic-hooray for a pair of organic Scotch whiskies. Highland Harvest Organic Scotch Whisky, made from a blend of three organic malts and an organic grain, is a fine choice for sipping in a glass with a few drops of water. Benromach Organic Speyside Single Malt Scotch Whisky is made from organic barley and yeast and is aged at least three years. It's rich and delicious, if pricey.

organic wine and champagne

Organic spirits may just be taking off, but organic wines— including bubbly—are already well established. And they're becoming more popular all the time.

Labeling on organic wines can be confusing. To be called organic in the United States, a wine must be made from organically grown grapes and produced according to organic manufacturing standards. Sulfites, which are used as preservatives and stabilizers, cannot be added to these wines. However, some wines that are categorized as being made from organic grapes may have sulfites added. The addition of sulfites is debated endlessly, but it's not as consequential as it might sound. Sulfites are a problem primarily for people who have a sensitivity to them or are allergic to sulfites—for them, consumption of sulfites can lead to serious health problems. For most people, a more important consideration is whether a winery makes good wine and does so as a responsible steward of its land.

Terms like "biodynamic" and "sustainable" can add to label confusion. Grapes grown using biodynamic farming methods typically have not been subject to pesticides and other artificial chemicals; this approach also attempts to consider celestial (i.e., astrological) influences on soil and plant development to achieve the best results. Meanwhile, wine producers that tout their sustainable agriculture practices are primarily focused on being able to make their products without causing severe or irreversible damage to the environment. However, there are no set standards for what it means for a wine to be made sustainably, so this designation is all but meaningless unless you're familiar with a winery's practices. In other words, it's more meaningful for a wine label to include the word "organic" than "biodynamic" or "sustainable."

The popularity of organic wines around the globe hasn't yet led to consensus on certification and labeling. Indeed, French wines—including the famed bubbly from France's Champagne region—can be labeled organic without certification. This doesn't mean they aren't organic. Many wineries forego getting their wines certified organic because, with regulations and definitions still being debated, doing so can be a costly hassle. Skeptical consumers may prefer to seek out wines dubbed organic by reputable organizations such as the International Federation of Organic Agriculture Movements or affiliated groups. Of course, a little research online can help unearth organic impostors. With so many organic wines available, it's hard to single out the best producers, much less individual bottles. Your best bet is to cultivate a relationship with a knowledgeable local wine merchant, who can point you to good organic wines.

other organic spirits and liqueurs

VeeV açai (pronounced ah-SIGH-ee) spirit is not certified organic, but its ingredients include organic American winter wheat and wild açai berries harvested from the Amazon rain forest. Açai is considered the preeminent "superfruit," containing 57 percent more antioxidants than pomegranates or blueberries and 30 times more heart-healthy anthocyanins than red wine. These dark berries also give this exotic spirit a delicate, floral cherry-and-licorice taste. Los Angeles–based VeeV is no slouch in its efforts to be green. A certified carbon neutral company, it uses wind-generated electricity to power its distillery, uses recycled paper packaging and soy-based inks on labels, and donates one dollar for each bottle sold to efforts to preserve the Brazilian rain forest.

Started by Californians Lisa Averbuch and Sabrina Moreno-Dolan in a loft apartment, the aptly named LOFT Organic Liqueurs produces certified organic spirits featuring the flavors of lavender, lemongrass, and spicy ginger. The company is also tinkering with seasonal flavors such as tangerine. Made in a manner similar to the Italian liqueur limoncello, LOFT liqueurs have a nicely balanced sweetness that makes them ideal as mixers or sipped cold and straight. They're currently available only in California, Oregon, and New York, as well as online.

organic mixers, sweeteners, and such

Tonic water, sodas, even prefab cocktail mixers traditionally made with corn syrup, dyes, and preservatives are getting the organic treatment. Modmix is one of the first certified organic cocktail mixers on the market, coming in summery flavors such as Citrus Margarita, Pomegranate Cosmopolitan, Wasabi Bloody Mary, Mojito, Lavender Lemon Drop, and French Martini (pineapple, raspberry, and a touch of lemon). All are made from filtered water, organic fruits and herbs, and unrefined cane sugar.

Several of the recipes in this book call for organic lemon or lime sour (also sold as "bar mix"). This currently isn't available commercially; here's a recipe so you can make your own.

lemon or lime sour

MAKES 2 CUPS

8 ounces Organic Simple Syrup (page 23)
8 ounces freshly squeezed organic lemon or
   lime juice

> Stir the simple syrup and citrus juice together until
> well combined. The mixture will keep, in an airtight
> container, in the refrigerator for up to 1 month.

Many grocery stores carry organic sodas. Blue Sky
Beverage Company makes a good organic ginger ale and
lemon-lime soda, as does Santa Cruz Organic. The best
organic sodas I've tried are Britain's Fever-Tree ginger ale,
bitter lemon, and lemonade sodas.

I also like Fever-Tree's tonic and soda waters.
Sweetened with cane sugar and flavored with Sicilian
lemons, African marigolds, and hand-pressed Tanzanian
orange oil, Fever-Tree's Indian Tonic Water has a
wonderfully clean and lively taste.

Unlike most tonic waters, which are sweetened with high
fructose corn syrup, Brooklyn-based Q Tonic gets its crisp
and clean taste from a touch of organic agave nectar, real
quinine from South American trees (many tonic waters
contain synthetic quinine), and lemon juice. And Q Tonic has
less than half the calories of most nonorganic tonic waters.

Sadly, if you want to enjoy organic maraschino cherries,
you'll have to patronize cutting-edge bars and restaurants
that make their own. Still, you don't have to settle for Day-
Glo orbs packed with artificial flavors and colors. All-natural
marasca cherries are a wonderful alternative. Luxardo,
the same company that makes maraschino liqueur, also
produces marasca cherries in syrup—or *marasche al frutto*—
made without preservatives or thickening agents. Harder
to find, but worth the effort, are imported wild amarena
cherries in syrup made by the Italian companies Fabbri and
Toschi. These exquisite, tart fruits, grown around Bologna,
Italy, are also great on ice cream.

For sweeteners, look for organic sugar and organic agave nectar (derived from the same plant used to make tequila). Organic sugar is more widely available, though honey-like agave nectar is catching up in popularity as a healthier alternative to sugar because of its lower glycemic index—which is especially attractive to those who must monitor their blood glucose levels. A number of brands are popping up. Organic tequila maker 4 Copas produces bottled organic agave nectar. You'll find organic agave nectar and sugar in most specialty-foods stores, as well as health-conscious chains such as Whole Foods Market or online.

Organic honey may sound like a good idea, but because of how bees make honey, it's almost impossible in the developed world to guarantee that any honey is organic. Honeybees typically forage within a 2- to 2½-mile radius of their colonies and can pick up any number of environmental contaminants during their travels. In addition, the USDA has no standards for certifying any honey as organic. Nevertheless, many honey producers label their honey as organic, and "organic honey" is widely available in specialty food stores and grocery chains. Your best bet for finding the highest-quality honey is to buy it from a farmers' market, where you can talk with the person who raised the bees and bottled the honey.

Most folks know how aloe vera soothes sunburned skin, but many may be unfamiliar with the health benefits of drinking it. Some alternative medicine experts claim that aloe vera juice's rich cocktail of minerals and vitamins helps the body in a number of ways, such as improving circulation, regulating blood pressure, strengthening the immune system, defending the body against bacteria, regulating blood sugar, and ridding the body of toxins. In cocktails, organic aloe vera can serve as a sweetener, with a more herbaceous taste than sugar or agave nectar.

The most common way to sweeten a cocktail is to add what is known as simple syrup. It's easy to make, so here is a recipe for an organic version. Prepare a batch and keep it on hand in the fridge.

organic simple syrup

MAKES 2 CUPS

1 cup organic granulated sugar
8 ounces water

Combine the sugar and water in a small saucepan and bring to a boil. Reduce the heat to low and stir until the sugar is dissolved. Remove from the heat and let cool to room temperature. The syrup can be stored, in an airtight container, in the refrigerator for up to 1 month.

organic brown sugar simple syrup
Substitute 1 cup firmly packed organic brown sugar for the granulated sugar.

shopping organic

Fresh organic fruits, vegetables, and herbs are no longer confined to big cities or specialty grocery stores. Many supermarket chains routinely carry organic produce. Farmers' markets and community-owned farm co-ops are also excellent sources. Organic herbs and spices are not yet as ubiquitous, though you'll find them in chains such as Whole Foods Market or online.

Many of the recipes in this book call for organic fruit juices. You can buy "freshly squeezed" organic juices of all kinds at your grocery store. But true fresh squeezed from your own kitchen is worlds better. Not only is the juice as fresh as you can get it, flavor-rich oils from the skin of the fruit are also released, imparting wonderfully nuanced flavors to your cocktails.

Determining whether something is truly organic can be confusing. For example, take eggs. Shopping for them never used to be so complicated. These days you're faced with eggs that are "certified humane" or "American humane certified," omega-3 fortified, cage free, free range, or any number of designations awarded by a constellation of federal and state agencies.

Here's all you need to remember: Pick eggs that are Grade AA (best quality) and have the USDA organic emblem, which means they meet the standards of the U.S. agriculture department's National Organic Program. This means that, among other things, the birds are kept cage free and with access to the outdoors, they are not given antibiotics (even if sick), and their food is free of animal byproducts and made from crops grown without the application of pesticides, fertilizers, and/or raw sewage and that haven't been irradiated or genetically engineered.

Eggs can still be organic if deemed so by an independent or state-run program, but verifying this can be more trouble than it's worth. The same goes for eggs bought at farmers' markets.

As with alcohol, a USDA organic label is the most reliable way to authenticate if produce is truly organic. Note: Make sure you wash any fruit or veggies before you use them in your cocktails. Organic doesn't mean germ free. And even organic fruits such as lemons and limes can get a spraying of wax at the store to add luster. If you're not sure if something's clean, wash it just in case.

kitting out the green bar

You'll be able to make any of the cocktails in this book (or most any drink, for that matter) with only a few basic tools and a small selection of glasses.

tools

No offense to James Bond fans, but shaking isn't always the best way to mix a drink. Not every drink should be shaken. A good guideline is that if a cocktail is supposed to look clear (like a martini), you should stir it. Otherwise, shake it. Shaking adds tiny bubbles to a drink, giving it a cloudy appearance.

For **cocktail shakers**, there are two basic options. One is a cobbler shaker, which often resembles a rocket ship from a 1950s comic book. Usually made of stainless steel,

it consists of a bottom receptacle and top cap that fits (or should fit) snugly to minimize spillage. This top piece typically comes with a built-in strainer. Cobbler shakers look nice on a shelf, but I prefer the Boston shaker, which works better and is easier to clean. It consists of a pint-size beer glass and a slightly larger stainless-steel cup that fits tightly over its top.

Wielding a Boston shaker can feel awkward at first. The first couple of times you use it, you may be afraid the two pieces will separate or that the whole contraption will slip from your wet hands and go flying across your kitchen. Take a breath. Just give the stainless-steel top a good smack to form a seal and hold both ends when you're ready to shake. Every cocktailian has his or her own shaking stance and rhythm. I like to hold the shaker head high, as if shaking a piggy bank. With a little practice you'll become a pro at it.

You'll also need a **strainer**. The easiest to use are those that fit atop a Boston shaker's stainless-steel top cup. These are known as Hawthorn strainers.

Muddlers are nothing more than specially made sticks— usually wood or plastic—used to mash, bruise, or otherwise squish ("muddle") an ingredient to release its flavor. About 6 inches long, a muddler looks like a miniature billy club.

A **zester** is a nice tool to have on hand. It's used to scrape flavorful strips of citrus peel from the fruit and works far better (and is much safer to wield) than a knife.

For extracting juices, you can make do with the dish-like kind of **reamer**, which works great for citrus fruits. But you'll be far happier getting a handheld **squeezer** with two levers, which does a good job of straining out seeds and pulp. Of course, if you happen to have a **pull-down** or **electric juicer**, that'll work fine, too.

A **small measuring cup**—with gradations as small as $1/8$ ounce—is essential. Glass measuring cups work fine, but I'm partial to OXO's plastic Good Grips Mini Angled Measuring Cups because you can easily see from above how much liquid is in them.

Other essentials include a **bar spoon**, though any long-handled, thin spoon will work, and a **paring knife** (basically a small, sharp knife for slicing lemons and other fruits and veggies). You'll also need a **small cutting board**, but chances are you already have one.

glassware

The right glass does two things—it helps a drink taste and look its best. You can put a lot of effort into finding the perfect glass for every kind of tipple. But for most purposes, you really only need a few types of glasses.

- **Martini glass.** This V-shaped glass is also known by the more generic name "cocktail glass." Resist the temptation to get any of the cartoonishly big martini glasses that so many restaurants have been using since the late 1980s. Martini glasses are meant to hold 4 to 5 ounces. If you want more than that, make another drink.

- **6- to 8-ounce rocks glass.** This is also known as an old-fashioned glass.

- **8- to 12-ounce Collins or highball glass.** (The highball glass is a little shorter and squatter than a Collins glass.)

- **Large wine glasses** for punches and sangrias.

Chilling a glass is as simple as it sounds. Fill a glass with ice—crushed is best because it will come in contact with more of the surface of the glass. When you're ready to use the glass, dump out the ice. Or instead of filling the glass with ice, you can pop the glass in the freezer for 5 to 10 minutes.

This may sound heretical to some, but I'm not a big fan of salted or sugared rims on drinks. Chances are, not everyone to whom you serve drinks is either. That's why I suggest you salt or sugar half the rim of a glass. This way, you get the cool visual effect and your guests can enjoy their drinks however they prefer.

To sugar or salt a rim, pour a thin layer of sugar or kosher salt (don't use iodized salt for this) onto a flat plate. Slice a lemon, lime, or other citrus fruit in half and rub a piece of it around the rim of the glass just enough to moisten it.

Upend the glass, dip the rim into the sugar or salt, lift up the glass, and you're ready to add your cocktail and serve.

ice 101

Cocktails wouldn't exist if not for ice, and good ice makes all the difference in the world. To me, there is no such thing as being too finicky about the ice you use in your cocktails. Using the right ice is critical to cocktail sucess. Make sure you use the type of ice specified in each drink recipe; use shaved ice in a recipe that calls for crushed, and you've got cold slop.

Your refrigerator's icemaker may crank out ice in the shape of half moons. Tip your drink back and those half moons suddenly become curved skis rushing down the slope of your glass only to smack into your front teeth or lips and cause your drink to run down the front of your shirt. To avoid this, invest in either a machine that produces real cubes—the bigger the cubes, the better—or go old school and make your ice with stackable ice trays. If your parents could be bothered to take the 10 seconds required to fill a tray with water, so can you.

Silicone ice cube trays work better than the more rigid plastic or metal ones. Use distilled, or at least filtered, water for ice-making. Not only will you ingest fewer impurities, you'll produce clearer ice cubes—which make for a prettier drink.

For drinks calling for cracked ice, simply wrap up some ice cubes in a kitchen towel and give the bundle several smart whacks with your muddler or a small hammer.

Chances are you don't have a freezer devoted only to ice, so your ice will be sharing space with all manner of frozen foods. Nothing kills the taste of a great organic cocktail quite like chicken-flavored ice cubes. Keep this from happening by covering your trays of water tightly with plastic wrap before putting them in the freezer.

A perfectly good alternative to making ice at home is to pick up a bag of ice cubes from your grocery store. Or, if money is no object, you could plunk down several thousand dollars to buy a Kold-Draft ice machine. The ice-making equivalent of a SubZero refrigerator, these machines do produce perfect ice cubes—big, hard blocks that rattle satisfyingly in a glass. And because they're colder and bigger than typical cubes, they don't melt as quickly—a quality that helps keep your drink from getting too diluted.

One last note: **Unless otherwise indicated, all of the recipes in this book make one drink.** There are a few exceptions in some chapters, and all of the drinks in the Punch and Pitcher chapter yield more than one serving. In these instances, the serving size is noted at the beginning of the recipe.

Cheers!

fresh
and
zesty

S timulate your taste buds with flavor combinations as vibrant as they are unexpected with these delightfully bright libations.

mysterious stranger

The sweet-and-sour flavor of tamarind is nicely softened by the smooth sweetness of Brazilian cachaça, but it's the rosemary, with its intriguing hint of pine and lemon, that really brings this drink together in a, well, mysteriously delicious way. You'll find tamarind concentrate in most specialty grocery stores and shops carrying Indian foods, though you may have to head to the Internet for organic versions.

2 ounces cachaça
1 ounce organic tamarind concentrate
$^1/_2$ ounce freshly squeezed organic lemon juice
10 to 15 organic rosemary leaves
$1^1/_2$ ounces organic ginger beer or ginger ale
1 sprig organic rosemary

Add the cachaça, tamarind concentrate, lemon juice, and rosemary leaves to an ice cube–filled cocktail shaker. Shake vigorously, then strain the mixture into a rocks glass. Top off with the ginger beer and garnish with the rosemary sprig.

peppered angus

In this drink, organic lemon marmalade takes healthy taste to a whole new, lip-puckering level. It also kicks this version of a pisco sour into the stratosphere of savory cocktails. Pisco is a grape brandy from South America. This drink gets its name (the "Angus," not the "peppered") from the British mixologist who created it.

1½ ounces pisco
1½ ounces fresh organic pineapple juice
1 tablespoon organic lemon marmalade
Dash of Angostura bitters
1 medium-size organic egg white (see Note)
Organic lemon twist
Freshly ground organic black pepper

Add the pisco, pineapple juice, marmalade, bitters, and egg white to an ice cube–filled cocktail shaker. Shake like the devil himself is chasing you. Strain the mixture into a chilled martini glass. Garnish with the lemon twist and top with two grinds of black pepper.

NOTE: Make sure your egg whites are very fresh, and do not serve this drink to the elderly or anyone with a compromised immune system.

flor de baya

Lime, cranberry, and vinegar provide a trio of bright but subtle notes of tartness in this drink.

2 ounces organic reposado tequila
$^3/_4$ ounce freshly squeezed organic lime juice
$^1/_2$ ounce Organic Simple Syrup (page 23)
$^1/_2$ ounce Organic Cranberry Gastrique
  (recipe follows)
1 organic lime wedge

Place a large handful of cracked ice in a cocktail shaker. Pour the tequila, lime juice, simple syrup, and gastrique over the ice. Shake vigorously, then strain the mixture into a chilled martini glass. Garnish with the lime wedge.

~~~~~~~~~~~~~~

organic cranberry gastrique

Combine 6 ounces organic white-wine vinegar, $^3/_4$ cup organic sugar, 5 ounces fresh organic cranberries, the juice and grated zest of half of an organic lemon, 1 organic star anise, and 2 organic whole cloves in a large saucepan. Bring to a boil, then continue to boil for 15 minutes, using a wooden spoon to help break up the cranberries. Strain the mixture through a cheesecloth-lined strainer (pressing to get as much liquid out of the solids as possible), let the liquid cool, place in an airtight container, and refrigerate. The mixture will keep in the refrigerator for up to 1 week.

spicy tangelo pisco sour

This drink offers a provocative combination of tart lime, sweet tangelo and hibiscus, and spicy green chile sauce—all delivered on a velvety magic carpet of egg white. Add a few extra dashes of the chile sauce if you're in the mood for more heat. Hints of vanilla and licorice in the Galliano provide an exotic accent. You can find the hibiscus syrup and organic green chile sauce in specialty food stores or online (see Online Resources, page 171).

1 organic tangelo (substitute 1 mandarin orange
   if tangelos aren't in season), unpeeled,
   quartered and seeds removed
2 organic lime wedges
$1/2$ ounce Galliano liqueur
$1/2$ ounce hibiscus syrup
$1^1/2$ ounces pisco
1 medium-size organic egg white (see Note)
Dash of Angostura bitters
Dash of organic green chile sauce
Organic tangelo twist

In a cocktail shaker, muddle the tangelo, lime wedges, Galliano, and hibiscus syrup until most of the juice has been squeezed out of the tangelo. Add the pisco, egg white, bitters, and chile sauce, and fill the shaker with ice cubes. Shake vigorously for about 20 seconds, then double-strain the mixture into a rocks glass filled with crushed ice. Garnish with the tangelo twist.

NOTE: Make sure your egg whites are very fresh, and do not serve this drink to the elderly or anyone with a compromised immune system.

jalisco flower

If orange juice is the only citrus acquainted with champagne in your home, your bubbly needs to get out more. Orange juice can sometimes smother the delicate flavor of champagne, but organic grapefruit juice's shiny acidity and more restrained sweetness, along with the smoothed edges of aged tequila and the floral charms of elderflower liqueur, really put champagne on a pedestal.

1 ounce freshly squeezed organic grapefruit juice
3/4 ounce elderflower liqueur
1/2 ounce organic reposado tequila
3 ounces organic champagne

Pour all of the ingredients except the champagne into an ice cube–filled cocktail shaker. Shake vigorously, strain the mixture into a champagne flute, then top with the champagne.

plaza passion

Tangy and fragrant, organic passion fruit is upfront with its intentions—which is just fine by the other ingredients in this opulent quencher.

7 organic mint leaves
1½ ounces organic tequila (either blanco or reposado)
1 ounce organic agave nectar
¾ ounce organic passion fruit puree (from a few thumb-size chunks of yellow or purple passion fruit)
¼ ounce Cointreau
¼ ounce freshly squeezed organic lemon juice
Splash of club soda
1 organic lemon wedge

In a cocktail shaker, muddle 6 of the mint leaves until bruised. Add the tequila, agave nectar, passion fruit puree, Cointreau, and lemon juice, and fill the shaker with ice cubes. Shake vigorously, then strain the mixture into a chilled highball glass. Top off with the club soda. Wrap the remaining mint leaf around the lemon wedge and secure with a toothpick. Balance the toothpick on the rim of the glass.

la nueva vida

The appeal of the cool sweetness of apples and glowing warmth of aged tequila is pretty obvious. But dry vermouth, so often gin's foil, does a nifty trick in this drink: It enhances the other flavors and rounds off their edges. If possible, use apple juice made from Fuji apples, which have a crisp, sweet taste.

2 ounces organic reposado tequila
1¹/₂ ounces organic apple juice
¹/₂ ounce dry vermouth
1 thin organic apple wedge, unpeeled

Pour the tequila, apple juice, and vermouth into an ice cube–filled cocktail shaker. Shake vigorously, then strain the mixture into a chilled martini glass. Garnish with the apple wedge perched on the rim of the glass.

coming in hot!

In this remarkably multifaceted drink, a few
teensy slivers of jalapeño transform what would
be a tasty but ho-hum strawberry margarita
into a modern classic. And while you're sipping,
try this trick: Concentrate on the taste of each
individual ingredient, and you will be able
to transport the jalapeño from the merest
suggestion of heat to center stage.

2 organic strawberries, hulled
4 slivers peeled and seeded organic jalapeño chile
$^3/_4$ ounce freshly squeezed organic lemon juice
$1^1/_2$ ounces organic reposado tequila
$^1/_2$ ounce organic agave nectar

In a cocktail shaker, muddle the strawberries, 3 of
the jalapeño slivers, and the lemon juice until well
mashed. Add the tequila and agave nectar, and fill
the shaker with ice cubes. Shake vigorously, then
strain the mixture into a chilled martini glass. Garnish
with the remaining jalapeño sliver.

spicy pepino

In this cocktail, jalapeño's heat is nimbly
tempered by the cilantro, with cucumber and
agave providing a cool sweetness that's nicely
restrained by the shot of lemon.

One 1/3-inch-thick round organic jalapeño chile
Three 1/2-inch-thick rounds peeled organic cucumber
1/4 cup organic cilantro leaves
1 1/2 ounces organic white rum
1 1/2 ounces freshly squeezed organic lemon juice
1/2 ounce organic agave nectar
1 thin slice organic lime

In a cocktail shaker, muddle the jalapeño until lightly
mashed. Add the cucumber and cilantro (saving
a single leaf for garnish) and muddle again until
everything is mashed. Add the rum, lemon juice, and
agave nectar and fill the shaker with ice cubes. Shake·
vigorously, then double-strain the mixture into a
chilled martini glass. Garnish with a lime slice on the
rim of the glass and float the remaining cilantro leaf
on the drink's surface.

pom pom margarita

Savory and tart, unsweetened pomegranate juice finds a perfect partner in the smokiness of aged tequila in this remarkably smooth take on the classic cocktail.

2 ounces organic reposado tequila
2 ounces organic pomegranate juice
$^1/_2$ ounce freshly squeezed organic lime juice
$^1/_2$ ounce organic agave nectar
Kosher salt (optional)

Pour all of the ingredients except the salt into an ice cube–filled cocktail shaker. Shake vigorously, then pour the mixture into 2 (salt-rimmed, if you like) martini glasses.

poolside

This libation has more depth than it would first appear. Chardonnay brings hints of apple, pear, and oak, while the lemon juice provides a nice acidity and the vodka gives some oomph.

8 organic seedless red grapes
1 ounce Organic Simple Syrup (page 23)
$^3/_4$ ounce freshly squeezed organic lemon juice
$1^1/_2$ ounces organic Chardonnay
1 ounce organic vodka

In a cocktail shaker, muddle the grapes, simple syrup, and lemon juice until the grapes are crushed. Add the Chardonnay and vodka, and fill the shaker with ice cubes. Shake vigorously, then strain the mixture into an ice cube–filled Collins glass.

saffron margarita

What a big difference the reddish-orange wisps of saffron make in this drink, suffusing an already delicious cocktail with an indescribable exotic flair. If you cannot find fresh mango, look for frozen mango puree in your supermarket freezer section.

1$^1/_2$ ounces organic tequila (either blanco
  or reposado)
$^1/_2$ ounce Cointreau
$^1/_2$ ounce freshly squeezed organic lime juice
1$^1/_2$ ounces organic mango puree (from
  about a handful of peeled mango chunks)
1 teaspoon organic agave nectar
Pinch of organic saffron threads
Kosher salt
1 thin slice organic lime (optional)

Combine the tequila, Cointreau, lime juice, mango puree, agave nectar, and saffron in an ice cube–filled cocktail shaker. Shake vigorously, then strain the mixture into a chilled martini glass with a salted rim; the threads of saffron will float in the drink. For extra color, garnish with a lime slice on the rim of the glass, if you like.

ginger-cilantro mule

Heady and healthful ginger appears in this drink in four different ways, harmonizing with fresh cilantro, lime, and aged tequila for an invigorating cocktail whose name invokes the 1950s drink the Moscow Mule. The intense flavor of ginger beer and a healthy shot of vodka were what originally provided the mule's "kick." This mule delivers a more civilized jolt from the subtle ginger flavors in Domaine de Canton liqueur.

2 thin slices peeled organic fresh ginger
2 teaspoons Ginger-Infused Organic Simple
   Syrup (recipe follows)
$1^1/_2$ ounces organic reposado tequila
$^3/_4$ ounce Domaine de Canton liqueur
1 teaspoon organic agave nectar
$^1/_2$ ounce freshly squeezed organic lime juice
Handful of organic cilantro leaves
Splash of organic ginger ale
1 thin slice organic lime

In a cocktail shaker, muddle the ginger and simple syrup until the ginger is mashed but not pulverized. Add the tequila, liqueur, agave nectar, lime juice, and cilantro, and fill the shaker with ice cubes. Shake vigorously, then strain the mixture into an ice cube-filled rocks glass and top with the ginger ale. Float the slice of lime on top.

~~~~~~~~~~~~~~~~~~~~~~~~~~~~~~~~~~~~~~

ginger-infused organic simple syrup

In a medium-size saucepan, combine $^1/_2$ cup organic sugar, 4 ounces water, and a thumb-size chunk of organic ginger, peeled and thinly sliced. Heat over low heat and let simmer for 15 minutes, stirring until the sugar dissolves. Remove from the heat and let cool. Strain out the ginger. The syrup can be stored, in an airtight container, in the refrigerator for up to 1 month.

If you already have some Organic Simple Syrup on hand and want to make an easier version of this, combine 1 ounce thinly sliced peeled organic ginger with 8 ounces Organic Simple Syrup (page 23) in a glass jar. Let sit for at least 2 hours, and preferably overnight, in the refrigerator. Strain out the ginger; the syrup will keep, in an airtight container, in the refrigerator for up to 1 month.

grilled pineapple–kiwi margarita

The sweetness of agave nectar and grilled pineapple balances the tartness of lime juice and kiwi fruit in this drink, with tequila providing the kick to wake it all up.

Half of an organic lime, cut in half
Half of an organic kiwi, peeled and cut in half
1 slice organic pineapple, grilled until golden brown and cut into pieces
1/2 ounce organic agave nectar
2 ounces organic tequila (either blanco or reposado)
Kosher salt

In a cocktail shaker, muddle the lime, kiwi, grilled pineapple, and agave nectar until the fruit is mashed but not pulverized. Add the tequila, and fill the shaker with ice cubes. Shake vigorously, then strain the mixture into a salt-rimmed, ice cube–filled old-fashioned glass.

pom-aniac

Big, brassy pomegranate and lively lemon find a counter beat in smooth maraschino cherry and cool cucumber, but it's that crucial splash of bitter Campari that really makes this symphony of flavors come together in delicious harmony.

2 ounces organic pomegranate juice
1½ ounces organic vodka
½ ounce freshly squeezed organic lemon juice
½ ounce organic agave nectar
Splash of Campari
½ ounce maraschino liqueur or Cointreau
Club soda or sparkling mineral water
1 or 2 thin rounds organic cucumber
Organic lemon twist

Pour the pomegranate juice, vodka, lemon juice, agave nectar, Campari, and maraschino liqueur into an ice cube–filled cocktail shaker. Shake vigorously for 30 seconds, then strain the mixture into an ice cube–filled glass. Top off with club soda and garnish with the cucumber round and lemon twist.

pear tea martini

This is a classic case of opposites attracting. Green tea, herbaceous and calming, really works with the zingy richness and floral qualities of the pear cider.

2 ounces Green Tea–Infused Organic Vodka
  (recipe follows)
2 ounces organic pear cider
1 slice organic pear, unpeeled

Combine the infused vodka and cider in an ice cube-filled cocktail shaker. Shake vigorously, then strain the mixture into a chilled martini glass. Gently drop in the pear slice.

green tea-infused organic vodka

Combine 1 teaspoon organic green tea leaves or 1 tea bag of organic green tea with 1 cup organic vodka and let steep for 2 hours. Strain (or remove the tea bag); the vodka will keep, in an airtight container, in a cool place or the refrigerator for up to 6 months.

gingered blackberry cooler

Tart, sweet, and savory all at once, this should be the official cocktail of late summer.

2 ounces organic vodka
1 ounce freshly squeezed organic lemon juice
$1/2$ ounce organic agave nectar
Dash of orange bitters
3 organic basil leaves
4 organic blackberries
Splash of organic ginger beer

Combine the vodka, lemon juice, agave nectar, bitters, basil, and 3 of the blackberries in an ice cube–filled cocktail shaker. Shake vigorously (no muddling here), then strain the mixture into an ice cube–filled highball glass. Top off with the ginger beer and serve garnished with the remaining blackberry.

mekong martini

In this drink, the lively, distinctive flavor of fresh cilantro plays to and tames the jalapeño's heat. Great on its own, this cocktail also pairs perfectly with spicy Asian food.

1 teaspoon chopped organic cilantro
Two $1/4$-inch-thick rounds organic jalapeño chile
$1^3/4$ ounces organic gin
1 ounce freshly squeezed organic lemon juice
$3/4$ ounce Organic Simple Syrup (page 23)

Combine all of the ingredients in an ice cube–filled cocktail shaker. Shake vigorously, then strain the mixture into a martini glass.

silkeborg cocktail

This drink is named for the Danish town famous for its aquavit, a spirit distilled from either potato or grain and flavored with various herbs. Elderflower and the spicy, nutty caraway in the aquavit complement each other wonderfully, with the tarragon vodka adding a spark of anise flavor.

3/4 ounce Tarragon-Infused Organic Vodka
   (recipe follows)
3/4 ounce aquavit
3/4 ounce freshly squeezed organic lemon juice
1/2 ounce elderflower liqueur
1/2 ounce Organic Simple Syrup (page 23)
1 organic mint leaf

Combine the infused vodka, aquavit, lemon juice, elderflower liqueur, and simple syrup in an ice cube-filled cocktail shaker. Shake vigorously, then strain the mixture into a chilled martini glass. Garnish with the mint leaf.

~~~~~~~~~~~~~~~~~~~~~~~~~~~~~

tarragon-infused organic vodka

Place several sprigs of organic tarragon in 4 ounces organic vodka. Let steep for at least 4 hours at room temperature. Remove the tarragon. The vodka will keep, in an airtight container, in a cool place or the refrigerator for up to 6 months.

sun gold zinger

Tangy but not too tart, this libation is almost improbably golden in color, thanks to the delicately sweet orange cherry tomatoes. It's delicious on the tongue—and to behold.

4 orange-hued organic cherry tomatoes
Generous pinch of organic sea salt
$1/2$ ounce freshly squeezed organic lemon juice
$1^3/_4$ ounces organic vodka
$1/4$ ounce organic agave nectar

In a cocktail shaker, muddle 3 of the tomatoes, the salt, and lemon juice until the tomatoes are mashed. Add the vodka and agave nectar, and fill the shaker with ice cubes. Shake vigorously, then strain the mixture into a chilled cocktail glass (a martini glass will show this drink off best). Garnish with the remaining tomato, speared on a toothpick and placed across the glass.

à la pêche

Peachy sweetness and the heat of jalapeño couldn't be more opposite flavors—or more delicious together. Toss in the freshness of cucumber and floral jasmine, and you've got a peach of a cocktail.

1 sliver organic jalapeño chile
Half of a very ripe organic peach, peeled, pitted, and cut into several pieces
1 ounce organic gin
1 ounce peach liqueur
$1/2$ ounce freshly squeezed organic lime juice
$1/2$ ounce Jasmine Green Tea-Infused Organic Simple Syrup (recipe follows)
1 thin round peeled organic cucumber

In a cocktail shaker, muddle the jalapeño until mashed. Add the peach and muddle until thoroughly mashed. Add the gin, peach liqueur, lime juice, and simple syrup, and fill the shaker with ice cubes. Shake vigorously, then strain the mixture into a chilled martini glass. Garnish by floating the cucumber slice on the surface of the drink.

jasmine green tea-infused organic simple syrup

Brew $1/2$ cup organic jasmine green tea (a stronger brew works best). In a small saucepan, combine the brewed tea with $1/2$ cup organic sugar. Bring to a boil, then reduce the heat to a gentle simmer and stir until the sugar is fully dissolved. Let cool to room temperature. The syrup can be stored, in an airtight container, in the refrigerator for up to 1 month.

caribbean sour

I'm not the first person to fall head over heels at first sip with rhum agricole, or agricultural rum. Arguably the most complex of rums, it's made from fresh, pure sugarcane juice—unlike many rums, which are made with molasses. The result is an exotically smoky, earthy flavor—a taste that many folks say, not surprisingly, tastes more organic. In this drink, rhum agricole is mixed with the same cane sugar used to make the rum, the honey-sweet juice of tangerines, tart lemon juice, and a dash of allspice liqueur, resulting in one strikingly sensuous drink.

The allspice liqueur is a rum-based concoction that is a staple of Tiki cocktails; it can be found in better liquor stores and online (see Online Resources, page 171). St. Elizabeth Allspice Dram, produced in Austria, is an excellent brand.

1 1/2 ounces rhum agricole
2 tablespoons organic sugar
3/4 ounce organic tangerine juice
3/4 ounce freshly squeezed organic lemon juice
1/4 ounce allspice liqueur
Organic tangerine twist

In an ice cube–filled cocktail shaker, combine the rum, sugar, citrus juices, and allspice liqueur. Shake vigorously for 5 to 10 seconds, then strain the mixture into an ice cube–filled old-fashioned glass. Garnish with the tangerine twist.

autumn's cup

It is true that this cocktail tastes best (read: fantastic) when the mercury is headed south come fall. But why wait all year to enjoy such a wonderful cocktail? Whenever you crave that September feeling, just stir yourself one of these, which combines a double dose of apple flavor with organic bay leaves and the subtle depth of the French herbal liqueur Benedictine, whose closely guarded recipe is said to contain more than two dozen all-natural herbs and spices. A splash of soda water sets it all dancing. Just be sure to warn your guests that the bay leaves and cloves are there for flavor, not for eating.

1¼ ounces Calvados
¾ ounce Benedictine liqueur
5 thin organic apple wedges, unpeeled
2 organic bay leaves
3 organic whole cloves
Splash of club soda
Pinch of freshly grated organic nutmeg

Combine the Calvados, Benedictine, apple, bay leaves, and cloves in a tall ice cube–filled glass. Stir, then top off with the club soda and a light grating of nutmeg.

lush and
fruity

e njoy the intense freshness of organic peaches, strawberries, blackberries, cherries, and other fruits showcased in these deliciously inviting drinks.

emperor norton's mistress

The Bogie and Bacall of booze, smoky bourbon
and provocatively flavorful organic strawberries
are a perfect pairing curiously improved by
the soft vanilla hints of the liqueur Navan and
the regal citrus zest of Cointreau. This drink
was named in honor of Joshua Norton, a turn-
of-the-nineteenth-century character from San
Francisco who proclaimed himself Emperor of
the United States. As his "mistress," this drink is
as delightfully eccentric as he was.

4 medium-size organic strawberries, hulled
1½ ounces bourbon
½ ounce Navan vanilla liqueur
¼ ounce Cointreau

In a cocktail shaker, muddle 3 of the strawberries
into juice. Add the bourbon, Navan, and Cointreau,
and fill the shaker with ice cubes. Shake vigorously,
then strain the mixture into an ice cube–filled old-
fashioned glass. Slice the remaining strawberry
halfway through and set on the rim of the glass.

watermelon aguafresca

MAKES 2 DRINKS

Watermelon's juicy ripeness and rum's sultry smokiness really bring out the clove-like spice of basil in this super-refreshing drink. And though watermelon conjures memories of Fourth of July picnics, it may be better suited to Valentine's Day. Scientists have found that this fruit isn't just a great source of vitamin C; it's also got ingredients that boost the libido. This is the perfect quaff to enjoy with your sweetie.

Handful of organic basil leaves, chopped
2 pinches of salt
6 ounces organic watermelon juice (about a
  heaping handful of seeded watermelon chunks,
  pureed and pushed through a strainer)
4 ounces organic rum
1 ounce Organic Simple Syrup (page 23)
½ ounce freshly squeezed organic lemon juice

In a cocktail shaker, muddle the basil, salt, and a splash of the watermelon juice until the basil is well bruised. Fill the shaker with ice cubes and add the remaining watermelon juice, the rum, simple syrup, and lemon juice. Shake vigorously, then pour the mixture, unstrained, into two Mason jars.

milk of millennia

This is a highly quaffable, not-so-sweet cocktail that really shows off the exotic cherry flavor of the açai, with bright notes of mint, ginger, and orange. One could argue that this drink is good medicine for what ails you, and certainly tastier than milk of magnesia!

3 thin slices peeled organic fresh ginger
6 organic mint leaves
$1/2$ ounce organic agave nectar
$1^{1}/_{2}$ ounces cachaça
$3/4$ ounce açai spirit
$1/2$ ounce freshly squeezed organic
   lemon juice
Organic orange twist

In a cocktail shaker, muddle the ginger and mint with the agave nectar until roughly mashed. Add the cachaça, açai spirit, and lemon juice, and fill the shaker with ice cubes. Shake vigorously, then strain the mixture into a chilled martini glass. Garnish by floating the orange twist on the surface of the drink.

nazca cocktail

Organic apple juice and grape juice enliven pisco's fermented grapes. But it's the vanilla in the simple syrup that provides this drink's smooth sophistication.

11 organic red grapes
1½ ounces pisco
1 ounce organic apple juice
1 teaspoon Vanilla-Infused Organic Simple Syrup (page 158)

In a cocktail shaker, muddle 8 of the grapes until mashed. Add the pisco, apple juice, and simple syrup, and fill the shaker with ice cubes. Shake vigorously, then strain the mixture into a chilled martini glass. Garnish with the remaining 3 grapes, speared on a toothpick and balanced on the rim of the glass.

pineapple caipirinha with sweet lime espuma

This cocktail is a zesty, airy confection that deftly uses contrasting textures—foam and firmness—to highlight how well lime, pineapple, and the sugarcane brandy cachaça play together.

Half of an organic lime, cut into 4 pieces
Four $\frac{1}{2}$-inch cubes organic pineapple
4 organic sugar cubes
1 ounce freshly squeezed organic lime juice
1 ounce organic agave nectar
1 large organic egg white (see Note)
2 ounces cachaça
1 spiky organic pineapple leaf (optional)

In a cocktail shaker, muddle the lime, pineapple, and sugar cubes until the mixture has an even consistency. In a separate small shaker, combine the lime juice, agave nectar, and egg white to make the espuma. "Dry shake" (shake without ice) until the mixture is thickly frothy, about 30 seconds. Add ice cubes to the muddled mixture and pour in the cachaça. Shake vigorously, then pour the mixture, unstrained, into a tall glass. Top with the espuma and garnish with the pineapple leaf, if using.

NOTE: Make sure your egg whites are very fresh, and do not serve this drink to the elderly or anyone with a compromised immune system.

blackberry mojito

The tart and minty mojito gets an enlivening kick from sweet organic blackberries in this new take on a traditional favorite.

4 organic blackberries
5 organic mint sprigs
1 organic lime, quartered
1$^1/_2$ ounces organic rum
Splash of organic lemon-lime soda

In a highball glass, muddle the blackberries, 4 of the mint sprigs, and 3 of the lime wedges until the berries are mashed. Add ice cubes to fill, then the rum, and stir. Top off with the soda. Serve garnished with the remaining lime wedge set on the rim of the glass and the mint sprig floating atop the drink.

tropical caipirinha

MAKES 2 DRINKS

The Caipirinha, a sublime mix of sugar, lime, and cachaça, is a marvel of simplicity. But one sip of this amped-up version of Brazil's national drink and you might wonder whether the country should consider awarding that honor to this tipple instead. It's that wonderful. Something about the exotic musky-tart quality of organic passion fruit and the sweet zing of strawberries really makes an already fantastic drink, well, even better.

4 organic lime wedges
4 organic strawberries, hulled and sliced
Half of an organic passion fruit, cut in half
  and the pulp scooped out
Half of an organic kiwi, peeled and cut into
  a few pieces
2½ teaspoons organic sugar
3½ ounces cachaça

In a cocktail shaker, muddle the lime wedges, strawberries, passion fruit pulp, kiwi, and sugar gently until the fruit is roughly mashed. Add the cachaça and fill the shaker with ice cubes. Shake vigorously, then pour the mixture, unstrained, into a rocks glass.

NOTE: Yellow passion fruit is generally bigger than the purple version, but the pulp of the purple fruit is often less acidic and richer in flavor and aroma.

w.c.c. fizz

Inspired by the Los Angeles Lakers' stunning NBA 2008 Western Conference Championship win, this drink's thematically correct purple and gold hues also make it stunning to look at. Try one. I bet you'll be a fan.

6 to 8 organic blackberries
1½ ounces organic reposado tequila
¾ ounce elderflower liqueur
¾ ounce freshly squeezed organic lemon
  juice
½ ounce Organic Ginger-Agave Syrup
  (recipe follows)
Splash of club soda
Pinch of grated organic lemon zest

Place the blackberries in a Collins glass. Fill the glass to the top with crushed ice and set aside. In a cocktail shaker, combine the tequila, elderflower liqueur, lemon juice, and ginger-agave syrup, and fill the shaker with ice cubes. Shake vigorously, then strain the mixture into the Collins glass. Top with the club soda and give a quick, gentle stir. Sprinkle the lemon zest over the surface of the drink.

~~~~~~~~~~~~~~~~~~~~~~~~~

organic ginger-agave syrup
Combine equal parts juiced organic fresh ginger (it's best to do this with a centrifugal juicer) and organic agave nectar. This will stay flavorful for 3 days; store in the refrigerator.

detox margarita

This drink makes for sound mind and body. That smooth and lightly sweet splash of aloe vera juice isn't just nicely balancing the heat of the tequila; it is also detoxifying your body. A note of caution: Aloe vera juice is also a laxative. In other words, you might not want to drink these all night long.

2 ounces Organic Lemon Sour (page 21)
1 ounce organic tequila (either blanco or
  reposado)
1 ounce organic aloe vera juice
1/2 ounce Cointreau
Splash of organic agave nectar
Splash of freshly squeezed organic lime juice
1 organic lime wedge

Combine the lemon sour, tequila, aloe vera juice, Cointreau, agave nectar, and lime juice in an ice cube–filled cocktail shaker. Shake vigorously, then strain the mixture into a martini glass. Garnish with the lime wedge set on the rim of the glass.

strawberry-basil martini

The sweet ripeness of strawberries is both showcased and tempered by the sweet-sour flavor of the balsamic reduction, creating a complex and refreshing cocktail.

3 organic strawberries, hulled
3 organic basil leaves
3 ounces organic vodka
1 ounce organic agave nectar
1 teaspoon Organic Balsamic Reduction
  (recipe follows)

In a cocktail shaker, combine all of the ingredients and muddle gently until the berries are mashed but not pulverized. Fill the shaker with ice cubes, then shake vigorously and strain the mixture into a chilled martini glass.

~~~~~~~~~~~~~~~~~~~~~~~~

organic balsamic reduction

Pour 8 ounces good-quality organic balsamic vinegar into a small, heavy saucepan and bring to a boil. Reduce the heat to a simmer and cook until the vinegar has the consistency of a thick syrup, about 20 minutes. Let cool before using. The reduction will keep, in an airtight container, in the refrigerator for up to 6 months. In a pinch, you can save time by substituting balsamic glaze, sold in specialty food stores and some supermarkets, for the reduction.

kiwi envy

Elderflower liqueur, with its almost indescribable complexity, picks up the kiwi and really supercharges it, and the gin provides the perfect canvas to capture it all.

4 thin slices peeled organic kiwi
$1^1/_2$ ounces organic gin
$^3/_4$ ounce elderflower liqueur
$^1/_2$ ounce freshly squeezed organic lime juice
$^1/_2$ ounce Organic Simple Syrup (page 23)
Splash of club soda
1 thin slice unpeeled organic kiwi

In a cocktail shaker, muddle the peeled kiwi slices until mashed but not so much that they become a paste. Add the gin, elderflower liqueur, lime juice, and simple syrup. Fill the shaker with ice cubes. Shake vigorously. Add the soda to the shaker, then strain into an ice cube–filled highball glass. To garnish, cut a notch in the unpeeled kiwi slice and set it on the rim of the glass.

caipirinha caramba

Brazil's classic cocktail gets dressed up when easygoing cachaça meets French bubbly. Black cherries lend a regal, exotic sweetness. This is my organic version of a recipe from Kim Haasarud's book *101 Champagne Cocktails* (Wiley, 2008).

3 organic black cherries, stems and pits removed
Half of an organic lime, cut in half
1 ounce Organic Simple Syrup (page 23)
1 ounce cachaça
3 ounces organic champagne
1 organic mint leaf

In a cocktail shaker, muddle the cherries, lime, and simple syrup until the fruit is thoroughly mashed. Add the cachaça, and fill the shaker with ice cubes. Shake vigorously, then pour the mixture into a chilled martini glass. Top off with the champagne and give a stir or two. Garnish with the mint leaf.

voluptuous

This is an arousing play of texture and taste. Egg white gives curvaceous structure to a drink that indulges so many desires—the lushness of strawberries, the passion of lemon, the exotic whimsy of anise. If you're really ambitious, dust the slice of strawberry with a pinch of organic fennel pollen for garnish. It adds a touch of heady, honey-like sweetness.

1 organic strawberry, hulled
$1/2$ ounce freshly squeezed organic lemon juice
$1^1/2$ ounces organic gin
Dash (really more like a few drops) of absinthe
1 medium-size organic egg white (see Note)
$1/2$ ounce organic agave nectar
1 slice organic strawberry

In a cocktail shaker, muddle the hulled strawberry and lemon juice until the berry is mashed. Add the gin, absinthe, egg white, and agave nectar, and fill the shaker with ice cubes. Shake vigorously for at least 15 seconds, then strain the mixture into a chilled martini glass. Float the strawberry slice on top of the drink.

TIP: To give the egg white a fluffier texture, put a thumb-size metal spring (the kind you'd find at a hardware store) in the shaker before shaking the mixture.

NOTE: Make sure your eggs are very fresh, and do not serve this drink to the elderly or anyone with a compromised immune system.

ki-why-not

Sweet-tart kiwi is the star of this wonderfully peppy cocktail.

Half of an organic kiwi, peeled and cut into
    several pieces
2 ounces organic gin
1$\frac{1}{2}$ ounces fresh organic pineapple juice
$\frac{1}{2}$ ounce freshly squeezed organic lemon juice
$\frac{1}{2}$ ounce Organic Simple Syrup (page 23)

In a cocktail shaker, muddle the kiwi enough to break it up well. Add the remaining ingredients, and fill the shaker with ice cubes. Shake vigorously, then strain the mixture into a chilled martini glass.

american beauty

Something about the juxtaposition of fresh fruit, bursting with temporal ripeness, brown sugar's notes of molasses, and the mellow warmth of aged whiskey gives this cocktail a depth of flavor that's delicious in any season.

5 organic blackberries
4 organic raspberries
4 organic blueberries
$^3/_4$ ounce Organic Brown Sugar Simple Syrup
   (page 23)
2 ounces rye whiskey or bourbon
1 ounce freshly squeezed organic orange juice

In a cocktail shaker, muddle the berries (reserving 1 blackberry for garnish) with the simple syrup until broken up. Add the rye and orange juice, and fill the shaker with ice cubes. Shake vigorously, then double-strain the mixture into a stemmed cocktail glass and garnish with the remaining blackberry, perching it on the rim of the glass.

golden gate fog

Never have I seen a drink so aptly named. A
cloud floats fog-like over this golden cocktail.
It takes just a sip to experience the eclectic mix
of delicately sweet organic white peaches and
the exotic, musky orange sharpness and spice
of Rhum Clément's Créole Shrubb liqueur—once
hard to find but increasingly available—and just
an intake of breath to savor the lively aromatics
of the mint garnish.

3 to 4 medium-size organic mint leaves
2 ounces organic white peach puree (from
  about a heaping handful of peeled organic
  white peach chunks)
$1/2$ ounce freshly squeezed organic lime juice
$1/2$ ounce Créole Shrubb orange liqueur
1 ounce absinthe
1 ounce ice water
1 sprig organic mint

In a cocktail shaker, lightly muddle the mint leaves.
Top with the peach puree, lime juice, and liqueur.
Stir well and set aside. In a small cup, combine the
absinthe and ice water. Fill a large wine glass half full
with ice cubes and strain the peach mixture over the
ice. Place a bar spoon on top of the wine glass so the
scoop faces the drink and gently pour the absinthe
mixture over the back of the spoon, "floating" this
liquid over the peach mixture and creating the "fog
over the Golden Gate." Garnish with the mint sprig
and serve with a swizzle stick.

bow thruster

As if the lush succulence of organic peaches and the husky warmth of bourbon weren't enough, Grand Marnier's rich, orangey sweetness and lemon's bright acidity create heaven in a rocks glass in this cocktail.

1$^1/_4$ ounces bourbon
1 ounce freshly squeezed organic
   orange juice
1 ounce Organic Lemon Sour (page 21)
$^1/_4$ ounce Grand Marnier
1 ounce organic peach puree (from about a
   handful of peeled peach chunks)
1 organic sweet cherry
Organic orange twist

Combine the bourbon, orange juice, lemon sour, Grand Marnier, and peach puree in an ice cube–filled cocktail shaker. Shake vigorously, then, without straining, pour into a rocks glass. Garnish with the cherry and orange twist.

black and tan

Not to be confused with the Guinness-based drink of the same name, this lovely libation combines the spicy flavors of rye and ginger with the beautiful freshness of organic fruits. Cool down a hot summer evening with this one.

7 organic blackberries
8 organic mint leaves
$1/2$ ounce Organic Simple Syrup (page 23)
$1/4$ ounce freshly squeezed organic lime juice
2 ounces rye whiskey
Splash of organic ginger beer

In a cocktail shaker, roughly muddle 5 of the blackberries and the mint leaves with the simple syrup and lime juice. Add the rye, and fill the shaker with ice cubes. Shake vigorously, then strain the mixture into an ice cube–filled Collins glass. Top with a healthy splash of ginger beer. Garnish with the remaining 2 blackberries threaded on a cocktail pick and balanced on the rim of the glass.

clean and classic

Organic ingredients shine in these simple yet sophisticated new twists on the best traditional cocktails.

prickly pear mojito

Organic prickly pear cactus may grow in places seemingly inhospitable, but its juice is anything but unwelcoming. Sweet and melon-like, the juice plays yin to the yang of the friskier ingredients in this luscious quencher.

You maybe able to find canned organic prickly pear juice, but just think how resourceful you'll look making it with fresh prickly pear. Choose fruit that gives slightly to palm pressure (don't worry, most stores remove the thorns first). The fruit should have a deep, even color. Ripen firm prickly pears at room temperature until soft. Peel them and remove the seeds with a spoon. Press the peeled fruit through a colander to remove any remaining seeds. Add an equal amount of water to this sweet, pulpy mass and chill until ready to use.

2 ounces organic rum
3 organic mint leaves
$1/2$ ounce freshly squeezed organic lime juice
$1/4$ ounce organic prickly pear juice, either
   canned or freshly squeezed
Splash of club soda

Combine the rum, mint, lime juice, and prickly pear juice in an ice cube–filled cocktail shaker. Shake vigorously, then strain the mixture into an ice cube–filled Collins glass. Top with the club soda and give a quick, gentle stir.

tahitian coffee

This cup of wonder takes coffee drinks to an ethereal level. The rich and flowery nuances of organic Tahitian vanilla, more complex than its pedestrian Bourbon-Madagascar bean relative, and the ambrosially delicate flavor notes of orange blossom honey make for a truly soothing cold-weather cocktail.

1 teaspoon organic orange blossom honey
1 teaspoon Tahitian Vanilla–Infused Organic
  Simple Syrup (recipe follows)
1 teaspoon organic butter
5 ounces brewed organic coffee
1½ ounces rhum agricole
Pinch of freshly grated organic nutmeg
Organic orange twist
1 organic cinnamon stick

Combine the honey, simple syrup, and butter in a coffee glass or mug. Add the hot coffee and stir until the butter melts and is incorporated. Add the rum, then grate the nutmeg over the top. Garnish with the orange twist and add the cinnamon stick as a stirrer.

tahitian vanilla–infused organic simple syrup

Slice 3 organic Tahitian vanilla beans in half lengthwise and, with the edge of the knife, scrape out the insides. In a small saucepan, combine ½ cup organic sugar, 4 ounces water, and the vanilla bean scrapings and vanilla pods. Bring to a boil, then reduce the heat to medium and stir until the sugar dissolves. Let cool to room temperature. Strain, then transfer to an airtight container. The syrup can be stored in the refrigerator for up to 1 month.

earl grey boxcar

Italian vermouth, English tea, and tropical rum combine for an eclectic, and harmonious, fresh take on this classic cocktail.

1½ ounces Earl Grey-Infused Organic Rum
   (recipe follows)
½ ounce Punt e Mes Italian vermouth (or other
   sweet red vermouth)
½ ounce fresh organic pineapple juice
½ ounce freshly squeezed organic lemon juice
½ ounce freshly squeezed organic lime juice
¼ ounce apricot brandy
Dash of Angostura bitters
1 thin slice organic lemon

Pour the infused rum, vermouth, fruit juices, brandy, and bitters into an ice cube–filled cocktail shaker. Shake vigorously, then strain the mixture into a martini glass and garnish with the lemon slice.

~~~~~~~~~~~~~~~~~~~~~~~~~~~

earl grey-infused organic rum
Combine 1 tea bag of organic Earl Grey tea and 8 ounces rum and let steep for 1 hour. Remove the tea bag, then pour the mixture into an airtight container. The infused rum can be stored in a cool place or refrigerated for up to 6 months.

grilled persimmon old fashioned

Grilling the persimmon gives this drink a nice smokiness and brings the sweetness of the fruit to the forefront. If you can find it, select a nonastringent variety of persimmon like Fuyu and make sure to use the fruit before it gets mushy.

1 organic persimmon, unpeeled
1 slice organic orange
5 generous dashes of Angostura bitters
1 heaping teaspoon organic brown sugar
2 ounces organic rum

Preheat a gas or charcoal grill. Cut the persimmon crosswise into 1/4-inch-thick slices. Remove the seeds with a small spoon or the tip of a knife. Grill the slices until soft and smoky, 3 to 4 minutes. Take the slices off the grill and let cool. (The grilled persimmon can be stored, in an airtight container, in the refrigerator for up to 1 week.) In a sturdy old-fashioned glass, muddle 1 slice of the grilled persimmon, the orange slice, bitters, and brown sugar until the fruit is crushed. Add the rum and stir with the muddler until the sugar dissolves. Add ice cubes and serve.

pear sidecar

I won't tell you that this drink can be made quickly, but the time spent is worth it. Watch the faces of your guests when they take the first sip. Better yet, check them out when they're finished. Of course, you probably won't want to see their reaction if you tell them there's no more.

Red wine, orange peel, and cinnamon accentuate the beautiful flavor of organic pear in this modern twist on a classic drink.

2 ounces pear brandy (Clear Creek's Williams
   Pear Brandy is very nice)
1 ounce Organic Pear-Infused Red Wine
   Reduction (recipe follows)
1 ounce freshly squeezed organic lemon juice
½ ounce organic agave nectar

In a cocktail shaker, combine all of the ingredients, and fill the shaker with ice cubes. Shake vigorously, then strain the mixture into a chilled martini glass.

organic pear-infused red wine reduction

In a large saucepan, combine one 750-milliliter bottle medium-bodied red wine, the peels of 2 organic oranges, 2 organic cinnamon sticks, and a pinch each of ground organic cardamom seeds and freshly grated organic nutmeg. Bring to a boil, then add 2 organic pears (sliced but not peeled) and continue to boil until the pears are soft. Using a slotted spoon, remove the pears and press them gently in a strainer to remove the pear juice; reserve the juice and solids. Reduce the heat under the saucepan to a simmer and add the pear skins and pulp back to the simmering wine. Stir occasionally as the wine slowly reduces. Just before the reduction becomes syrupy (about 45 minutes), add the pear juice and reduce again until syrupy (about 10 minutes). By adding the pear juice at the end, its flavor will remain prominent. Let cool; strain before using. The mixture can be stored, in an airtight container, in the refrigerator for up to 1 week.

organic agave margarita

There's nothing tricky about this one; it's just an organic version of your basic margarita recipe. But this cocktail's organic ingredients—and the use of agave nectar instead of Cointreau—make for a simple drink of great and intense flavors.

2 ounces organic tequila (either blanco or
  reposado)
1½ ounces freshly squeezed organic lime juice
1 ounce organic agave nectar
Kosher salt (optional)
1 thin slice organic lime

Combine the tequila, lime juice, and agave nectar in an ice cube–filled cocktail shaker. Shake vigorously, then strain the mixture into an ice cube–filled (and salt-rimmed, if you like) cocktail glass. Set the lime slice on the rim of the glass.

hot buttered maple rum

Organic maple syrup replaces the traditional brown sugar here, imparting a wonderfully smoky smoothness to this cold-weather warmer.

1 teaspoon organic maple syrup (Coombs
  Family Farms makes good stuff)
1 teaspoon organic butter
1 organic cinnamon stick
2 organic whole cloves
3 ounces organic dark rum

In a small saucepan, bring about ½ cup of water to a boil. In a mug, combine the maple syrup, butter, cinnamon, and cloves. Pour in the rum and stir (the mixture should fill the mug about halfway). Fill with boiling water and stir well. Serve immediately.

lunacy

Despite its name, this is a drink that's wonderfully well balanced. Here's where organic berries— the riper, the better—really shine. The delicate smoothness of açai spirit, made from the Amazonian berry of the same name, and the crisp, winey quality of the Lillet Blanc don't so much tame the riot of flavor from the blackberries as showcase it.

5 organic blackberries, plus a few extra for garnish
$^3/_4$ ounce freshly squeezed organic lemon juice
$^1/_2$ ounce Organic Simple Syrup (page 23)
1$^1/_2$ ounces organic reposado tequila
$^3/_4$ ounce Lillet Blanc
$^3/_4$ ounce açai spirit

In a cocktail shaker, muddle the blackberries, lemon juice, and simple syrup until the berries are mashed. Add the tequila, Lillet Blanc, and açai spirit, and fill the shaker with ice cubes. Shake vigorously, then strain the mixture into an ice cube–filled rocks glass and garnish with a few fresh blackberries.

lavender lemon drop

Lavender's sweet aroma of fresh-cut wood gives just the right counterpoint to the tartness of the citrus vodka and lemon juice. This is a bright and shiny drink.

2 ounces organic citrus vodka
1 ounce freshly squeezed organic lemon juice
1 ounce Lavender-Infused Organic Simple
   Syrup (recipe follows)
Organic sugar
Organic lemon twist

Combine the vodka, lemon juice, and simple syrup in an ice cube–filled cocktail shaker. Shake vigorously. Sugar the rim of a chilled martini glass, then strain the mixture into the glass. Garnish with the lemon twist.

lavender-infused organic simple syrup

In a medium-size saucepan, combine 4 ounces water, $1/2$ cup organic sugar, and $1/2$ cup organic lavender flowers (fresh are best, but dried are easier to find—just make sure they're organic), crushed and wrapped securely in cheesecloth. Warm over medium heat, stirring, until the sugar dissolves; be careful not to let it boil. Remove from the heat, let cool, strain out the flowers, and pour into an airtight container. Refrigerate overnight before using. The syrup, which has a light pink color from the lavender, will keep in the refrigerator for up to 2 weeks.

If you already have some Organic Simple Syrup on hand, here's an easier version: In a glass jar, combine a handful of organic lavender sprigs with 8 ounces Organic Simple Syrup (page 23). Let sit for at least several hours (a full day in the fridge is best), then remove the sprigs.

h.w. version 2.0

This is a souped-up version of the Harvey Wall-banger. The high-octane flavors of orange and lemon combine with silky-smooth vanilla-hinted gin to create a flashy creamsicle of a cocktail.

2 ounces Vanilla Bean–Infused Organic Gin
  (recipe follows)
$^3/_4$ ounce freshly squeezed organic lemon juice
$^1/_2$ ounce freshly squeezed organic orange juice
$^1/_2$ ounce Galliano
$^1/_2$ ounce Organic Simple Syrup (page 23)
2 drops of orange flower water
Organic orange twist

In a cocktail shaker, combine all of the ingredients except the orange twist, and "dry shake" (shake without ice) for 10 seconds. Add ice cubes and shake for another 10 seconds. Strain the mixture into an ice cube–filled Collins glass. Garnish with the orange twist.

vanilla bean–infused organic gin

Place 1 split organic vanilla bean in 6 ounces organic gin and let infuse for 48 hours. Remove the vanilla bean, then pour the infused gin into an airtight container. The mixture can be stored in a cool place or refrigerated for up to 6 months.

nobody's darling

Aromatically herbal, angelica root teams up here with the almost floral taste of yellow Chartreuse to help make one tasty tipple. You can find angelica root in health food stores and specialty food stores such as Whole Foods Market.

2 ounces organic gin
1 ounce Angelica Root–Infused Organic Honey
  (recipe follows)
$^3/_4$ ounce organic celery juice (about one hand-
  length of a stalk sent through a juicer)
$^1/_2$ ounce yellow Chartreuse
$^1/_2$ ounce freshly squeezed organic lemon juice
One 3-inch-long organic lemon twist

Combine the gin, infused honey, celery juice, Chartreuse, and lemon juice in an ice cube–filled cocktail shaker. Shake vigorously, then strain the mixture into a chilled martini glass. Garnish with the lemon twist.

~~~~~~~~~~~~~~~~~

angelica root–infused organic honey

In a medium-size saucepan, pour 10 ounces boiling water over 2 ounces dried angelica root enclosed in a tea ball and let infuse for 45 seconds to 1 minute. Remove the tea ball. Add $^1/_2$ cup organic honey to the angelica "tea." Simmer over low heat until the mixture reduces by two-thirds, about 1 hour, stirring occasionally. Let the mixture cool. The infused honey can be stored, in an airtight container, in the refrigerator for up to 2 weeks.

french 75

Organic ingredients are the sole updates this classic cocktail needs. And rightfully so—tart lemons and sugar's sweetness are borne aloft on the champagne bubbles, with just the right herbaceous oomph. You can make this drink with simple syrup, but there is something about the snow-globe effect of superfine sugar that really adds to this drink's dreamy quality.

Be warned: This drink wasn't named after a French World War I artillery gun for nothing. It may be as airily refreshing as a summer's dream, but it packs a wallop. After two of these, you may develop a French accent. After three, you'll be fluent (or think you are).

2 ounces organic gin
1 teaspoon organic superfine sugar or
3/4 ounce Organic Simple Syrup (page 23)
1/2 ounce freshly squeezed organic lemon juice
3 to 4 ounces organic champagne or sparkling wine

In a cocktail shaker, combine the gin, sugar, and lemon juice, and fill the shaker with ice cubes. Shake vigorously, then strain the mixture into a Collins glass half full of ice cubes. Top with the champagne, give a gentle stir or two, and serve immediately.

purple basil gimlet

Besides being more intensely flavorful than its emerald-hued relative, purple basil also provides an enticingly faint lilac hue in this stunner that you'll enjoy looking at almost as much as you'll love drinking.

2 ounces organic gin
1/2 ounce freshly squeezed organic lime juice
1/2 ounce organic agave nectar
5 organic purple basil leaves

Combine the gin, lime juice, agave nectar, and 4 of the basil leaves (reserve the smallest one for garnish) in an ice cube–filled cocktail shaker. Shake vigorously, then strain the mixture into a chilled martini glass. Float the remaining basil leaf on top of the drink.

bellini au naturel

Yes, I'm talking about the same drink that has launched a thousand brunches. But when made with the ripest, sweetest organic white peaches, this classic cocktail really shows why we should all toast its invention at Harry's Bar in Venice, Italy, in 1943. An authentic Bellini calls for the slight sweetness of light-bodied Italian Prosecco instead of drier champagne.

1 organic white peach, peeled, pitted, and pureed
3 to 4 ounces organic Prosecco

Pour the peach puree into a champagne flute. Slowly—very slowly—pour in the Prosecco until the glass is full. If the puree hasn't fully mixed with the Prosecco, give one or two gentle stirs.

kentucky christmas

Organic cranberries play to and off of bourbon's sweetness for a wonderfully refreshing way to enjoy the taste of Christmas, even in summer (use frozen cranberries if fresh are not available).

Handful of organic cranberries, rinsed and
  picked over
4 ounces organic cranberry juice
2 ounces bourbon

In a pint glass, muddle the cranberries until crushed (make sure not to pulverize the cranberries so much that you release the seeds' bitter taste). Add a large handful of cracked ice, the cranberry juice, and bourbon, and stir.

churchill downs

Apples and bourbon are like old friends—at ease, well matched, able to finish each other's sentences. But sometimes familiarity can be a little boring. Adding the soft sweetness of grapes helps showcase all that's great about these two—and brings a welcome freshness.

10 to 15 organic grapes (green, red, or a
  combination)
1 ounce bourbon
$1/4$ ounce freshly squeezed organic lemon juice
Splash of organic apple juice

In an old-fashioned glass, muddle the grapes gently until mashed. Add the bourbon, lemon juice, and apple juice, fill the glass with ice cubes, and stir.

roasted red pepper julep

Organic red peppers, jam-packed with flavor when raw, transform into culinary gold when subjected to fire. The smoke and caramel released by roasting them accentuate those same characteristics in the bourbon. The mint and sparkling water give the drink just the right freshness and restraint.

4 sprigs organic mint
1 ounce Organic Simple Syrup (page 23)
2 ounces Organic Roasted Red Pepper Puree
  (recipe follows)
2 ounces bourbon
2 ounces cold sparkling water

In a Collins glass, muddle 3 sprigs of the mint and a dash of the simple syrup until the mint is bruised. Add ice cubes until the glass is halfway full, then add the remaining simple syrup, the red pepper puree, bourbon, and sparkling water. Stir slowly. Serve garnished with the remaining sprig of mint.

~~~~~~~~~~~~~~~~~~~~~~~~~~~~~

organic roasted red pepper puree

You can buy organic roasted red peppers, but fresh are better. Here's how to make your own:

Preheat the broiler. On a foil-lined roasting pan, place 1 large organic red pepper. Set under the broiler, turning it as needed until the skin is charred all over, 10 to 15 minutes. Remove from the oven and let cool. Peel off all the skin, cut out the stem, and scrape out the seeds. Process the pepper flesh in a food processor until smooth.

heirloom tomato g&t

As names go, heirloom just doesn't do justice to the riot of flavors these tomatoes pack. Some are as sweet as a peach; others are bracingly sharp, like citrus. Thankfully, nature gives some clues: Orange and yellow tomatoes, generally lowest in acid, are the sweetest. Green and white ones lean toward acidic and tart. Dark red and black varieties typically strike a balance in between.

There's no right or wrong type of heirloom tomato to use for this drink, though you'll probably want to start with something in the middle of the taste spectrum. Better yet, go with a touch of each extreme. Sweet will nicely offset tart for this perfect expression of summer.

3 ounces chopped organic heirloom tomatoes (about a heaping handful; no need to remove seeds)
2 ounces (a big handful) organic herb leaves, such as basil, dill, thyme, tarragon, or chives— whatever you like and looks good at the market
Half of an organic lime, quartered
1 1/2 ounces organic gin
Generous splash of organic tonic water
Kosher salt and coarsely ground organic black pepper (optional)

In a pint or other tall glass, muddle the tomatoes, herbs, and lime quarters together until the tomatoes are mashed but not pulverized. Add the gin, tonic water, and a large handful of ice cubes and stir. Serve in a chilled martini glass, rimmed with salt and pepper, if you like.

from the
garden

make your mother happy and drink your fruits and vegetables with these earthy refreshers brimming with the green goodness of the garden.

cherry tomato daiquiri

No, the name of this cocktail isn't a misprint. Tomatoes, especially when fresh and organic, are bursting with sweet fruit flavor, which makes them ideal for that quintessential sweet and sour cocktail, the daiquiri.

4 organic cherry tomatoes
2 ounces organic rum
1 ounce freshly squeezed organic lime juice
1 ounce Organic Simple Syrup (page 23)
Dash of Angostura bitters

In a cocktail shaker, muddle 3 of the tomatoes until broken apart. Add the rum, lime juice, simple syrup, and bitters, and fill the shaker with ice cubes. Shake vigorously, then strain the mixture into a chilled martini glass. Float the remaining cherry tomato in the drink.

green tea mojito

The health benefits of green tea are well known. But what may not be as celebrated is how well it works with mint and rum to make a remarkably refreshing summer thirst quencher.

1 tablespoon freshly squeezed organic lime juice
4 large organic mint leaves
2 teaspoons organic sugar
3 ounces brewed organic green tea, cooled to
   room temperature
1 ounce organic white rum

In a Collins glass, muddle the lime juice, mint, and sugar together until the mint is bruised. Fill the glass three-quarters full with ice cubes, pour in the green tea and rum, and stir well.

coming up roses

Rose petals and champagne make for an impossibly delicate cocktail treat here. Lime and rum provide a perfect background to the rose petals, rose syrup, and rose water. New York City cocktail consultant Junior Merino, who created this drink, uses Bacardi Razz, a raspberry-infused rum, in his version, but I've made it organic here. See Online Resources (page 171) for sources for organic rose water and rose syrup.

3 fresh organic rose petals
Half of an organic lime, cut into wedges
$^1/_2$ ounce organic rose syrup
2 to 3 drops of organic rose water
1$^1/_2$ ounces Raspberry-Infused Organic Rum
  (recipe follows) or Bacardi Razz rum
2 ounces organic champagne

In a cocktail shaker, muddle the rose petals, lime, rose syrup, and rose water until the petals are bruised. Fill the shaker with ice cubes, and add the infused rum. Shake vigorously, then strain the mixture into an ice cube–filled highball glass and top off with the champagne.

~~~~~~

raspberry-infused organic rum
In a glass jar, combine $^3/_4$ cup organic raspberries with 8 ounces organic white rum. Gently muddle until the berries are mashed. Let sit overnight, then double-strain the mixture into an airtight container. The infused rum can be stored in the refrigerator for up to 1 month.

fresh basil margarita

Here's a drink that would also be nice with zingy mint, but basil's spicier herbal flavor really makes this cocktail shine. The basil also wakes up your appetite.

4 to 6 organic basil leaves
1 ounce freshly squeezed organic lime juice
1 ounce organic agave nectar
1½ ounces organic tequila (either blanco
  or reposado)

In a cocktail shaker, muddle the basil, lime juice, and agave nectar until the basil is bruised. Add the tequila, and fill the shaker with ice cubes. Shake vigorously, then strain the mixture into an ice cube–filled rocks glass.

relic

At first sip, you'll swear it's the fresh organic peaches that make this drink taste so fantastic. But without the minty spice of the basil, this drink wouldn't be half as wonderful.

3 slices organic peach, unpeeled
3 organic basil leaves
1 ounce freshly squeezed organic lemon juice
1¾ ounces organic reposado tequila
½ ounce organic agave nectar

In a cocktail shaker, muddle the peach slices, 2 of the basil leaves, and the lemon juice until well mashed but not to a paste. Add the tequila and agave nectar, and fill the shaker with ice cubes. Shake vigorously, then strain the mixture into an ice cube–filled rocks glass. Float the remaining basil leaf on the surface of the drink.

green garden

English cucumbers have fewer seeds than regular cukes, which makes them less bitter. They are perfect for this springtime (or anytime) cocktail, which uses tequila, lime, and agave nectar to cleverly accentuate the cucumber. A splash of Moscato d'Asti adds the slightest hint of bubbles and a lightly fruity taste reminiscent of honeydew melons. A garnish of edible flowers gives the illusion of a floating spring flower garden.

1½ ounces organic blanco tequila
½ ounce Cucumber-Infused Organic Simple
  Syrup (recipe follows)
¼ ounce freshly squeezed organic lime juice
1 ounce organic Moscato d'Asti
Several edible organic flowers (such as small
  roses or lavender blossoms)

Combine the tequila, simple syrup, and lime juice in an ice cube–filled cocktail shaker. Shake vigorously, then strain the mixture into a chilled martini glass or champagne saucer. Add the Moscato d'Asti and garnish with the flowers.

cucumber-infused organic simple syrup

Juice 1 English cucumber (leave the skin on for flavor and color). Place the juice in a small glass bowl with an equal volume of Organic Simple Syrup (page 23) and 1 teaspoon freshly squeezed organic lime juice, and stir to combine. The syrup will keep, in an airtight container, in the refrigerator for up to 1 month.

copper pot

The rich flavors of apple and tequila perform a curious alchemy to imbue this drink with the most delicious hints of nuts and spices. The recipe calls for Calvados, a French apple brandy that's subtler and fruitier than American applejack.

2 ounces organic blanco tequila
1 ounce organic apple juice
½ ounce Calvados
½ ounce freshly squeezed organic lemon juice
½ ounce Organic Simple Syrup (page 23)

Combine all of the ingredients in an ice cube–filled cocktail shaker. Shake vigorously, then strain the mixture into a chilled martini glass.

alibi

While apricots work wonderfully in this drink, I prefer to use pluots, that tasty hybrid of plum and apricot. Their complex flavor—more plum than apricot—and more prominent sweetness pair well with the intensity of aged tequila and the remarkably complementary kick of garlic.

One-quarter of an organic pluot or apricot,
   unpeeled
1 organic garlic clove
½ ounce freshly squeezed organic lemon juice
1¾ ounces organic reposado tequila
¼ ounce organic agave nectar

In a cocktail shaker, muddle the pluot, garlic, and lemon juice until mashed. Add the tequila and agave nectar, and fill the shaker with ice cubes. Shake vigorously, then strain the mixture into an ice cube–filled rocks or Collins glass.

lady sage

This is a perfect example of how the simplest cocktails can also be the best. Herbaceous, aromatic sage and zesty lemon arrive on a magic carpet of smooth foam.

2 organic sage leaves
2 ounces organic gin
³/₄ ounce freshly squeezed organic lemon juice
³/₄ ounce Organic Simple Syrup (page 23)
1 medium-size organic egg white (see Note)

In a cocktail shaker, gently muddle one of the sage leaves until lightly bruised. Add the gin, lemon juice, simple syrup, and egg white. "Dry shake" (shake without ice) vigorously for a few seconds. Fill the shaker with ice cubes, and shake vigorously for another 6 seconds. Strain into a chilled martini glass. "Spank" the remaining sage leaf by placing it in the palm of one of your hands and giving it a single, hard slap to release the herb's aromas. Gingerly float the leaf in the center of the drink.

NOTE: Make sure your egg whites are very fresh, and do not serve this drink to the elderly or anyone with a compromised immune system.

elderflower fizz

The delicate floral qualities of the elderflower get a perfect uplift from the fizz of the champagne in this sparkler. This drink is also heightened by a vivid touch of lime softened by the sweetness of agave nectar. But what really makes this cocktail so heavenly are the devilishly diminutive leaves of a single sprig of organic thyme, as alluring as the trace of perfume from a passing girl.

1 ounce Organic Lime Sour (page 21)
$1/2$ ounce organic vodka
$1/2$ ounce elderflower liqueur
Splash of organic agave nectar
2 to 3 ounces organic champagne
1 sprig organic thyme

Combine the lime sour, vodka, elderflower liqueur, and agave nectar in an ice cube–filled cocktail shaker. Shake vigorously, then strain the mixture into a champagne flute or old-fashioned glass. Top off with the champagne. Place the sprig of thyme in the palm of one hand and "spank" it with the other to release its oils, drop it into the drink, then stir the cocktail once or twice before serving.

rain forest
ginger-green-tea-ni

Eco-conscious celebs such as Salma Hayek and Orlando Bloom have been spied sipping this drink at San Francisco's Azie restaurant. And for good reason. The earthiness of the tea-infused vodka is buoyed and balanced by the zesty zing of lime juice and the smoky orange flavor of Cointreau. The ambrosially sweet agave nectar used in this drink boasts a very low glycemic load (meaning it won't raise your blood sugar as much as table sugar does).

2 ounces Ginger and Green Tea–Infused
   Organic Vodka (recipe follows)
1¹/₂ ounces freshly squeezed organic lime juice
¹/₂ ounce organic agave nectar
¹/₄ ounce Cointreau
Tiny pinch of organic lime zest

Combine the infused vodka, lime juice, agave nectar, and Cointreau in an ice cube–filled cocktail shaker. Shake vigorously for 15 seconds, then strain the mixture into a martini glass. Using a cocktail zester, grate a tiny amount (1 to 2 passes) of lime zest over the top and serve.

ginger and green tea–infused organic vodka
Submerge 1 tea bag of organic green tea and 1 tea bag of organic ginger tea in 8 ounces organic vodka and let infuse for several hours (but no more than 5 hours) at room temperature. Remove the tea bags and pour the infused vodka into an airtight container. The vodka can be stored in a cool place or refrigerated for up to 6 months.

arboretum

Tangy cherry and orange mix and mingle with the herbal qualities of Chartreuse and crisp cucumber. You can substitute Cointreau for the maraschino liqueur, but I prefer maraschino's bright cherry zing. One sip and you'll understand the name; this drink is a garden in a glass.

2 ounces organic vodka
1 ounce green Chartreuse
$\frac{1}{2}$ ounce maraschino liqueur
$\frac{1}{2}$ ounce organic agave nectar
Splash of orange bitters
5 organic basil leaves (4 cut into thin strips,
   1 left whole)
1 thin round peeled organic cucumber

Combine the vodka, Chartreuse, maraschino liqueur, agave nectar, bitters, and basil strips in a cocktail shaker, and add a large handful of crushed ice. Shake vigorously for about 1 minute, then strain the mixture into a chilled martini glass. Garnish by floating the cucumber round and whole basil leaf atop the drink.

spiked blueberry-thyme lemonade

This drink can give you a summery feeling even if the mercury is headed below zero. Sweet and tart lemonade and lush blueberries team up for a luxuriantly refreshing cocktail. This is a perfect choice for outdoor parties or cookouts. Organic lemon thyme is inexplicably difficult to find in most grocery stores, but it's sold in some nurseries. However, the best way to get it is to grow it yourself.

8 organic blueberries, picked over for stems
4 sprigs organic lemon thyme
$^3/_4$ ounce Organic Simple Syrup (page 23)
$1^1/_4$ ounces organic vodka
1 ounce spring water
$^1/_2$ ounce elderflower liqueur
$^1/_2$ ounce freshly squeezed organic lemon juice
$^1/_4$ ounce yellow Chartreuse

In a cocktail shaker, muddle the blueberries, 3 of the thyme sprigs, and the simple syrup until the berries are mashed. Add the vodka, spring water, elderflower liqueur, lemon juice, and Chartreuse, and fill the shaker with ice cubes. Shake vigorously, then strain the mixture into a tall ice cube–filled glass. Garnish with the remaining sprig of thyme.

au provence

Fresh tarragon gives this cocktail a wonderfully subtle anise-like freshness, evocative of Provence and its delectable cuisine.

2 ounces organic vodka
1 ounce Tarragon-Infused Organic Simple
   Syrup (recipe follows)
³/₄ ounce freshly squeezed organic lime juice

Combine all of the ingredients in an ice cube–filled cocktail shaker. Shake vigorously, then strain the mixture into a chilled martini glass.

~~~~~~

tarragon-infused organic simple syrup

Combine ½ cup organic sugar and 4 ounces water in a medium-size saucepan. Simmer over medium heat, stirring, until the sugar dissolves. Remove from the heat, place a small bundle of fresh organic tarragon in the syrup, cover, and let steep for 20 to 30 minutes, until you have the desired intensity of flavor. Remove the tarragon. The syrup can be stored, in an airtight container, in the refrigerator for up to 2 weeks.

eden

"Floral and spicy flavors playing Twister" is the best way I can describe the playful intermingling of tastes happening in this cocktail. Cucumber's perfume pairs well with elderflower liqueur, with horseradish giving a curiously complementary kick.

1½ ounces organic cucumber vodka
½ ounce freshly squeezed organic lemon juice
½ ounce elderflower liqueur
½ ounce Organic Brown Sugar Simple Syrup
    (page 23)
1 tablespoon organic prepared horseradish
1 small, thin round peeled organic cucumber,
    salted

Combine the vodka, lemon juice, elderflower liqueur, simple syrup, and horseradish in an ice cube–filled cocktail shaker. Shake vigorously, then double-strain the mixture into a highball glass filled with crushed ice. Garnish with the salted cucumber round set on the rim of the glass.

vanderbilt avenue martini

Something about the taste of sage makes a cocktail feel more dressed up, though cucumber says casual to me. Put them together, add hints of flowers and pineapple, and you've got a drink that tastes and feels just as comfortably refreshing in a lawn chair by the pool as in a luxury penthouse. This drink's name comes from the address of the New York bar, The Campbell Apartment, in which it was first mixed and served.

2 fresh organic sage leaves
1 ounce organic cucumber vodka
$^3/_4$ ounce fresh organic pineapple juice
$^1/_2$ ounce elderflower liqueur
Organic Vanilla Bean-Infused Sugar (recipe follows)

In a cocktail shaker, gently muddle one of the sage leaves (but don't mangle it). Add the vodka, pineapple juice, and elderflower liqueur, and fill the shaker with ice cubes. Shake vigorously, then strain the mixture into a martini glass rimmed with the infused sugar (see below). Place the remaining sage leaf in the palm of one hand and "spank" it with the other to release its aroma. Float the leaf in the center of the drink as a garnish.

organic vanilla bean-infused sugar

In a sealable container, bury 2 to 3 organic vanilla beans, each slit lengthwise with a paring knife, in $^1/_2$ cup organic raw sugar. Allow to sit overnight, covered, at room temperature. Remove the vanilla beans from the sugar and pour the infused sugar into a small saucer. Moisten the rim of a cocktail glass with a small slice of lemon or lime, then invert the glass and dip it into the sugar.

beet-nyk

Alcoholic borscht this ain't. Organic yellow beets
have a wonderful natural sweetness that marries
well with the fruity flavor of apples and the
acidity of lemons, the dill tying them all together.
And the sweetness beets offer is healthy as
well—they are packed with antioxidants.

Make sure you use apple liqueur for this, not
the apple schnapps used to make apple-tinis.
Apple liqueur can be hard to find in stores; look
for it online.

2 pieces beet from Beet-Infused Organic
   Simple Syrup (recipe follows)
2 small sprigs organic dill
1¹/₄ ounces apple liqueur
1 ounce organic vodka
1 ounce Beet-Infused Organic Simple Syrup
   (recipe follows)
¹/₂ ounce freshly squeezed organic lemon juice

In a cocktail shaker, muddle the pieces of beet and 1
sprig of the dill until the beet is well mashed. Add the
apple liqueur, vodka, simple syrup, and lemon juice,
and fill the shaker with ice cubes. Shake vigorously,
then double-strain the mixture into a chilled martini
glass, tapping the strainer to help the liquid pass
through the beet pulp. Float the remaining sprig of
dill on the surface of the cocktail as a garnish.

beet-infused organic simple syrup

Remove the stems and leaves from 2 small organic yellow
beets, place the beets in a medium-size saucepan filled with
water, and bring to a boil. Continue to boil until the beets
are soft enough to pierce easily with a fork. Drain and let
cool, then slip the skins off the beets. Rinse the beets under
running water to clean off any debris, then cut them into
1-inch pieces and place in a container large enough to hold
the beets in a single layer. Pour in 4 ounces Organic Simple

Syrup (page 23), add the juice from 1 organic lemon, and give the mixture a couple of stirs. Let the beets infuse in the liquid for about 30 minutes in the refrigerator. Strain out the beets (save them to use in the drink; refrigerate until ready to use). The syrup can be stored, in an airtight container, in the refrigerator for up to 1 month.

lily pond

No mere garnish here, radish's peppery bite nicely complements the botanicals in the gin and cucumber. Crisp and clean, this will make you feel cool all over.

Two ¼-inch-thick rounds peeled organic cucumber
One-third of an organic lime, cut into 3 pieces
Half of an organic radish, thinly sliced
¼ ounce Organic Simple Syrup (page 23)
2½ ounces organic gin
1 ounce organic lemon-lime soda

In a cocktail shaker, muddle 1 of the cucumber rounds, the lime, radish, and simple syrup until the cucumber and radish are mashed but not pulverized. Add the gin, and fill the shaker with ice cubes. Shake vigorously, then strain the mixture into a highball glass and top off with the soda. Garnish by floating the remaining cucumber round on top of the drink.

jessica rabbit

Ginger and carrot, such a great pair on the plate, jump the bar here and hop into a cocktail glass. Sexy, spicy ginger, ingénue carrot, and swank basil make for one palate-perking and visually voluptuous cocktail. You can find organic candied or crystallized ginger at specialty food stores like Whole Foods Market or online.

2 thumb-sized pieces organic candied or
  crystallized ginger
1 organic basil leaf
1$1/2$ ounces organic vodka
2 dashes of sweet vermouth
$1/2$ ounce organic carrot juice
$1/2$ ounce Ginger-Infused Organic Simple
  Syrup (page 48)

In a cocktail shaker, muddle one piece of the candied ginger and the basil roughly. Add the vodka, vermouth, carrot juice, and simple syrup, and fill the shaker with ice cubes. Shake vigorously, then strain the mixture into a chilled martini glass. Garnish by floating the remaining piece of candied ginger on top.

snap-pea-irinha

This one is smart and crisp. The herbal notes of the peas marry nicely with the gin's botanicals, with tart lime keeping things lively. And the snap peas are an excellent source of vitamin B_6 and folic acid, which are great for memory and mood. Mom and Dad would be so proud of you for eating your vegetables.

$1/4$ cup organic snap peas, ends trimmed
1 organic lime, cut into 8 wedges
1 ounce Organic Simple Syrup (page 23)
$1^1/_2$ ounces organic gin
Coarsely ground organic black pepper

In a cocktail shaker or tall glass, combine the snap peas, lime wedges, and simple syrup and muddle thoroughly. Add the gin and a handful of crushed ice and stir, then pour the mixture, unstrained, into a rocks glass. Garnish lightly with pepper (one crank of the pepper mill is plenty).

sweet pea

With their scent of spring and sweet flavor, English peas (fresh, organic ones, that is) make a perfect companion for floral elderflower liqueur and tart-sweet grapes.

9 organic English peas (there are about 3 peas
   per pod; in a pinch, substitute 1 teaspoon
   organic pureed peas)
10 organic seedless green grapes
1 teaspoon organic brown sugar
1 ounce organic gin
$1/2$ ounce elderflower liqueur
$1/4$ ounce freshly squeezed organic lime juice

In a cocktail shaker, muddle 6 of the peas, the grapes, and brown sugar until the grapes and peas are mashed. Add the gin, elderflower liqueur, and lime juice, and fill the shaker with ice cubes. Shake vigorously for 10 seconds, then double-strain the mixture into a chilled martini glass. Garnish by floating the remaining 3 peas in the drink.

meditation

Cocktail hour is a magical time to relax, unwind, and, with that most civilized ritual of preparing and enjoying a favorite drink, put the day's worries behind you. Few drinks can deliver tranquility and taste like this one. The becalming aroma of lavender and soothing cucumber unite with assertively herbaceous Chartreuse (made by monks dedicated to a lifelong pursuit of peace) and botanically beatific gin to create harmony in a glass.

2 thin rounds peeled organic cucumber
2 ounces organic honeydew melon juice (made
   by pureeing a couple of handfuls of honeydew
   chunks and pushing them through a strainer)
1 ounce freshly squeezed organic lime juice
1½ ounces organic gin
¾ ounce Lavender-Infused Organic Simple Syrup
   (page 101)
½ ounce green Chartreuse
2 dashes of organic rose water (see Online
   Resources, page 171)
1 marble-size ball organic honeydew melon
One 3-inch-long spear peeled organic cucumber

In a cocktail shaker, muddle the cucumber slices, melon juice, and lime juice until the cucumber is lightly mashed. Add the gin, simple syrup, Chartreuse, and rose water, and fill the shaker with ice cubes. Shake vigorously, then strain the mixture into an ice cube–filled Collins or wine glass. Garnish with the honeydew melon ball on a toothpick and the cucumber spear set on the rim of the glass.

bride of celery

Poor celery. In cocktails, you're always a brides-maid, never the bride. Here, this perennial gar-nish is now wearing the gown and strutting her stuff in a perfect marriage of celery's crisp, herbal flavor and the sweetness of apples.

One-quarter of an organic Granny Smith
  apple, unpeeled, cored and diced
One 3-inch stalk organic celery, chopped
$1/2$ ounce freshly squeezed organic lemon juice
2 teaspoons organic sugar
$1^1/2$ ounces organic gin
$1/2$ ounce organic apple juice
1 organic celery leaf

In a cocktail shaker, muddle the apple and celery with the lemon juice and sugar until roughly mashed. Add the gin and apple juice and give it a little stir to mix the flavors well. Fill the shaker with ice cubes. Shake vigorously, then double-strain into a chilled martini glass. Garnish the drink with the celery leaf, floating it on the top or inside edge of the glass.

secret garden

This is a terrible name for this drink. I mean, anyone who tries it will blab. Oh, they'll prattle on about how preposterously well balanced it is, how wonderful the zingy sweetness of the grapefruit tastes with those hints of sugared cilantro and cucumber and gin, and . . . oh, see what I mean?

2$\frac{1}{2}$ ounces organic gin
1 ounce freshly squeezed organic grapefruit juice
$\frac{1}{2}$ ounce Cilantro-Infused Organic Simple Syrup
 (recipe follows)
$\frac{1}{4}$ ounce freshly squeezed organic lime juice
1 thin round peeled organic cucumber

Combine the gin, grapefruit juice, simple syrup, and lime juice in an ice cube–filled cocktail shaker. Shake vigorously, then strain the mixture into a chilled martini glass. Garnish with the cucumber round perched on the lip of the glass.

cilantro-infused organic simple syrup

In a glass jar, combine a handful of organic cilantro leaves with 8 ounces Organic Simple Syrup (page 23). Let sit for at least several hours (a full day in the fridge is best), then strain out the cilantro. The syrup can be stored, in an airtight container, in the refrigerator for up to 2 weeks.

punch
and
pitcher

you and your guests will have plenty to be festive about with these crowd-pleasing concoctions.

bank exchange punch

MAKES 6 DRINKS

This updated take on pisco punch may be better than the original, whose popularity in late 1800s San Francisco rivaled the nation's recent, far less rational, crush on the Cosmo. Its name is a nod to the Bank Exchange, a San Francisco saloon where its predecessor was first poured. This punch takes full advantage of the tangy, grapey sweetness of pisco—a grape brandy from South America—and fresh, tart lemons. New to the mix are the luscious sweetness of pineapple and a touch of allspice liqueur, a treat redolent of clove, cinnamon, and nutmeg, which wakes up and warms up all of the ingredients.

12 ounces pisco
6 ounces Pineapple-Infused Organic Simple
   Syrup (recipe follows)
3 ounces freshly squeezed organic lemon juice
1/3 ounce allspice liqueur (St. Elizabeth Allspice
   Dram is my favorite)
6 small chunks fresh organic pineapple

In a pitcher, combine the pisco, simple syrup, lemon juice, allspice liqueur, and a large handful of ice cubes. Stir until chilled (you want the ice to melt just a bit for the proper dilution). Serve in old-fashioned glasses or punch glasses (wine glasses will do in a pinch) and garnish each drink with a chunk of pineapple.

pineapple-infused organic simple syrup

Combine several small chunks of peeled organic pineapple with 6 ounces Organic Simple Syrup (page 23) and let infuse overnight in the refrigerator. Strain and store in an airtight container. The syrup will keep in the refrigerator for up to 1 month.

dark and stormy

MAKES 4 DRINKS

Old cocktails are getting revived today faster
than the undead in a zombie movie. This one
has been resurrected—and improved—with the
livelier flavors of organic orange, fresh ginger
juice, and an invigorating splash of sparkling
Italian bubbly.

8 ounces organic spiced or dark rum
8 ounces freshly squeezed organic orange
   juice (preferably from super-sweet Valencias)
6 ounces freshly squeezed organic lime juice
4 ounces organic agave nectar
1 tablespoon organic ginger juice (see Note)
$1/8$ teaspoon ground organic cloves
About half of a 750-milliliter bottle organic
   Prosecco

Combine all of the ingredients, except the Prosecco,
in a pitcher and stir well. Chill until ready to serve.
When ready to serve, fill 4 Collins glasses with ice
cubes. Pour about $1/2$ cup of the mixture into each
glass and top off with the Prosecco.

NOTE: To get your ginger juice, start with a 2-inch
piece of organic fresh ginger. Grate the ginger on a
fine Microplane grater, wrap the grated ginger in a
piece of cheesecloth, and wring out the juice.
Alternatively, you can run the ginger through a
juicer, preferably a centrifugal juicer.

berry good sangria

MAKES ABOUT 7 DRINKS

You might like knowing, as you sip this drink, about a recent scientific discovery: Adding alcohol to strawberries and blackberries actually increases their antioxidant capacity. I prefer instead to let my mind drift, borne aloft on clouds of heavenly berry flavors, invigorating orange, and the lip-smacking tannins of red wine. Inspired by a recipe from Kim Haasarud's book *101 Sangrias & Pitcher Drinks* (Wiley, 2008), this version amps up the berries.

1 cup each of any three of the following organic
    berries: blueberries, strawberries (hulled and
    sliced), blackberries, boysenberries, or raspberries
6 ounces Organic Simple Syrup (page 23)
One 750-milliliter bottle organic red wine (any
    medium-bodied red will do)
8 ounces freshly squeezed organic orange juice
4 ounces triple sec
4 ounces organic vodka

In a medium-size saucepan, combine the berries and simple syrup over low heat. Stir constantly until the berries just begin to soften and discolor. Combine the wine, orange juice, triple sec, and vodka in a large pitcher. Add the berry mixture and stir well. Cover and refrigerate for at least 4 hours or overnight. Serve poured over ice cubes in large wine glasses.

watermelon cooler

The sweet tartness of the pomegranate liqueur balances smartly with snappy gin and flavor-packed watermelon. This is a great drink to serve at a patio party.

20 ounces organic watermelon juice (about half of a large watermelon, seeded, pureed, and pushed through a strainer)
10 ounces organic gin
10 ounces pomegranate liqueur (organic, if you can find it)
40 quarter-size organic watermelon or honey-dew melon balls made with a melon baller
6 ounces sparkling water

Combine the watermelon juice, gin, and pomegranate liqueur in a large pitcher and stir. Add the watermelon balls, then top with the sparkling water. Serve on the rocks in Collins glasses.

açai-lum sangria

As if the smooth and exotic cherry hints of açai
berries weren't enough, açai spirit is packed with
antioxidants, including many times more heart-
healthy anthocyanins than are found in red wine.
The versatility of açai spirit is on full display
in this drink; it softens the brightness of the
Sauvignon Blanc and grapefruit and lightens the
molasses tang of the brown sugar.

12 ounces açai spirit
12 ounces organic Sauvignon Blanc
2 ounces freshly squeezed organic grapefruit juice
10 dashes of Angostura bitters
1 ounce Organic Brown Sugar Simple Syrup
   (page 23)

Combine all of the ingredients in a pitcher, stir, and
serve over ice in tall glasses.

melon sangria

MAKES ABOUT 6 DRINKS

This is a preposterously easy and tasty cocktail. Summery melon supercharges the already melon-y Vouvray wine. Bitters add just the right complexity, with club soda lending a nice effervescent lift to it all. The result is a refreshing—and gorgeous—summer drink.

24 ounces chilled organic off-dry Vouvray wine
3 ounces club soda
12 dashes of Fee Brothers Grapefruit Bitters
  (easy to find in better liquor stores and online)
36 chilled organic melon balls (12 each of
  honeydew, watermelon, and cantaloupe)

In a pitcher, combine the wine, club soda, and grapefruit bitters. For each serving, place 6 of the melon balls (2 of each kind) in a large wine glass and pour in the sangria.

frozen sangria rita

MAKES 4 DRINKS

The key to this drink's considerable charm is choosing an organic Merlot with soft tannins and a modest alcohol level, so that it caresses rather than clobbers the pomegranate and blueberries.

4 ounces organic Merlot
4 ounces organic reposado tequila
4 ounces organic pomegranate juice
4 ounces freshly squeezed organic lime juice
4 ounces Organic Lemon Sour (page 21)
2 ounces Cointreau
2 ounces organic agave nectar
12 organic blueberries, picked over for stems
4 thin slices organic lime

In a blender, combine all of the ingredients except the lime slices, and blend with several handfuls of ice cubes. Serve in chilled rocks glasses with a lime slice set on the rim of each glass.

passion fruit sangria

MAKES ABOUT 7 DRINKS

Lip-puckering passion fruit and Riesling team up with tangerine and pineapple for a drink that's a little tart, a little sweet, and completely refreshing. Ginger and cloves give it a pleasantly earthy finish.

One 750-milliliter bottle organic dry Riesling wine
2 cups organic passion fruit puree (from about 6 passion fruit)
16 ounces fresh organic pineapple juice
Several whole organic cloves
1 organic lemon, cut into wedges
1 organic tangerine, cut into wedges
1 organic lime, cut into wedges
8 ounces organic ginger beer

In a pitcher or punch bowl, combine the wine, passion fruit puree, pineapple juice, and cloves. Cover and chill in the refrigerator overnight. When ready to serve, add the fruit wedges and ginger beer and serve over ice cubes in wine glasses or rocks glasses.

perfect whiskey punch

MAKES 10 DRINKS

This drink takes a classic punch recipe—we're talking 1817 classic—and gives it a gustatory goosing with the addition of dry vermouth and orange bitters. But what makes this punch, well, perfect is the addition of pineapple syrup, made from fresh organic pineapples and organic cane sugar.

20 ounces rye whiskey
10 ounces dry vermouth
5 ounces sweet vermouth
5 ounces Pineapple-Infused Organic Simple
   Syrup (page 147)
20 dashes of orange bitters
10 thin slices organic orange
Pineapple chunks from the simple syrup

Combine the rye, vermouths, simple syrup, and bitters in a punch bowl and stir. Add the orange slices and pineapple chunks. Serve in ice cube–filled double old-fashioned glasses, making sure to include an orange slice and piece of pineapple in each drink.

a.m. punch

A.M. does not mean this is for breakfast (not
that it wouldn't be an excellent way to start your
day). Rather, the A.M. refers to the initials of the
cocktail creator and his girlfriend, who . . . oh,
never mind. What's important is that this is a
wonderful drink for autumn and winter, and a
fantastic choice for holiday parties. The aged
tequila has a nifty cinnamon accent that's lovely
with the apple brandy.

7$1/2$ ounces organic añejo tequila
7$1/2$ ounces bonded (100 proof) applejack
7$1/2$ ounces elderflower liqueur
7$1/2$ ounces freshly squeezed organic lemon juice
5 ounces Vanilla-Infused Organic Simple Syrup
   (recipe follows)
10 ounces club soda
10 long organic cinnamon sticks

Combine the tequila, applejack, elderflower liqueur,
lemon juice, and simple syrup in an ice cube–filled
pitcher and stir well. Pour the mixture over a large
block of ice (you can get your block of ice by
freezing water in a plastic container or a bundt cake
pan) set in a punch bowl. Top off with the club soda.
To serve, ladle the punch into cups and give each
guest a cinnamon stick to use as a stirrer.

~~~~~~~~~~~~~~~~~~~~~~~~~~~~~~~~~~~~~

vanilla-infused organic simple syrup
With a knife, split 1 organic vanilla bean in half lengthwise,
then scrape out the insides of the pod. In a glass jar,
combine the pod and scrapings with 5 ounces Organic
Simple Syrup (page 23). Let infuse for at least 2 hours in
the refrigerator (overnight is better). Remove the vanilla
bean pod and transfer the syrup to an airtight container.
The syrup will keep in the refrigerator for up to 1 month.
Makes enough for one batch of punch.

zesty tom

Here's a drink that really lives up to its name. Mind you, zesty is not a synonym for "hot as hell." Rather, each element of this Bloody Mary–inspired drink brings just the right degree of fresh and spicy vigor to make one damn fine, and zesty, cocktail.

12 large organic heirloom tomatoes
6 small organic jalapeño chiles, plus 6 more
   for garnish (garnish optional)
6 large cloves organic garlic
Several pinches of organic sea salt
6 ounces organic vodka

Roast the tomatoes and 6 of the jalapeños on the grill or under the broiler until charred. Peel the blackened skin from the tomatoes and jalapeños. Make sure to get off as much of the skin as possible, or the juice will be bitter. Meanwhile, in a 400°F oven, roast the garlic until soft, about 35 minutes. Place the roasted tomatoes and jalapeños in a blender. Add the roasted garlic, squeezing it out of its skin. Blend until smooth, then strain the chile-charged tomato juice into a pitcher and add the salt. To make the drinks, fill a tall glass three-quarters full with ice cubes, then add 1 ounce of the vodka and fill with the tomato juice. If you like, garnish each drink with a jalapeño.

green and white summer sangria

MAKES 14 DRINKS

This easy-to-make sangria is light and slightly fruity—but not too sweet. And few things will be as welcome to guests as being handed this colorful, refreshing, eco-friendly libation as they walk through the door.

¾ cup hulled and halved organic strawberries, plus 14 more organic strawberries, hulled and partially cut in half
¾ cup roughly chopped peeled organic kiwi
¾ cup roughly chopped organic peaches
1 tablespoon organic wildflower honey
8 ounces organic peach nectar
4 ounces organic vodka
4 ounces açai spirit
Two 750-milliliter bottles organic Sauvignon Blanc

Finely chop the ¾ cup strawberries, the kiwi, and the peaches and place them in an airtight container (don't cover it just yet). Drizzle with the honey, then add the peach nectar, vodka, and açai spirit. Cover and let marinate for several hours in the refrigerator. When ready to serve, spoon 1 tablespoon of the fruit mixture and 1 ounce of the chilled liquid into each of 14 wine glasses. Fill the glasses with ice cubes, then top with the wine. Garnish by perching a strawberry on the rim of each glass.

cherry snaps

MAKES ABOUT 12 DRINKS

Like its name says, this party pleaser is a snap to prepare—but you'll need to let it steep overnight to reach its most glorious flavor. Rich and earthy organic black cherries lose their inhibition when partnered up with bourbon, and the ginger lends an enlivening zing.

One 750-milliliter bottle Maker's Mark bourbon
6 cups organic black cherries, stems and pits removed
4 ounces Ginger-Infused Organic Simple Syrup (page 48)

In a large pitcher, combine all of the ingredients, stirring to mix well. Cover and refrigerate overnight. When ready to serve, pour the mixture into ice cube–filled rocks glasses, making sure to include a few cherries in each drink.

frozen berry bellini

MAKES 4 DRINKS

In a perfect world, ice cream trucks would traverse all neighborhoods, offering kids organic ice cream—and adults this drink, freshly blended. Fresh berries, champagne, and a touch of organic pineapple juice that sets all the flavors dancing on your tongue make this a perfect frozen summer treat.

1 cup mixed organic berries (such as blackberries, strawberries, blueberries, and raspberries), plus extra berries for garnish
4 to 6 ounces organic champagne
2 ounces Organic Simple Syrup (page 23)
2 ounces fresh organic pineapple juice
2 cups ice cubes

Combine all of the ingredients in a blender and blend until smooth. Pour into small juice or rocks glasses and garnish each glass with a few berries.

sangri-la

This is a nifty riff on a white sangria recipe from Kim Haasarud's book *101 Sangrias & Pitcher Drinks* (Wiley, 2008). Fresh organic red and white grapes amplify the typically austere fruit of dry white wine, with the tangy sweetness of blood orange juice and triple sec nicely balanced by the lip-puckering tartness of green apple. A touch of cucumber and sage gives it all a welcome clean, herbaceous touch.

One 750-milliliter bottle organic dry white wine
16 ounces freshly squeezed organic blood orange juice
4 ounces triple sec
1 organic green apple, unpeeled, cored and sliced
1 cup organic red and white grapes, halved
One-quarter of an organic cucumber, peeled
  and thinly sliced into rounds
1 organic lemon, thinly sliced into rounds
1 organic lime, thinly sliced into rounds
32 ounces organic lemon-lime soda
8 organic sage leaves (optional)
8 small clusters of organic grapes (preferably
  champagne grapes; optional)

Combine the wine, blood orange juice, triple sec, apple slices, grape halves, cucumber rounds, lemon slices, and lime slices in a large pitcher and stir well. Cover and refrigerate for at least 4 hours (overnight is best to allow the flavors to develop). Pour the sangria into chilled glasses, about three-quarters full. Top with the soda. Garnish each glass with a sage leaf and/or grape cluster, if desired.

cherry chiller
MAKES ABOUT 5 DRINKS

The invigorating tartness of pureed lemons and
the lush ripeness of fresh cherries make for one
irresistible cocktail.

30 organic sweet cherries, stems and pits
    removed
5 ounces Organic Simple Syrup (page 23)
10 ounces organic gin
5 ounces Organic Lemon Puree (recipe follows)

In a pitcher, muddle the cherries and simple syrup
until the cherries are mashed. Add the gin and lemon
puree and stir. Strain the mixture into ice cube–filled
highball glasses.

~~~~~~~~~~~~~~~~~~~~

organic lemon puree
Chop 3 organic lemons (with their peels). Place in a
medium-size saucepan with 1/2 cup raw organic sugar
and 4 ounces water. Cook over low heat until the
lemons are soft, about 45 minutes. Puree the mixture
in a blender or food processor until smooth, and
strain through a fine-mesh strainer into an airtight
container, adding a pinch of salt. The puree can be
stored in the refrigerator for up to 1 week.

146 highland terrace punch

MAKES 7 TO 8 DRINKS

I like to think of this drink as a kind of super Caipirinha. The already festive trio of cachaça, cherries, and pineapple finds fresh ways to celebrate with the floral hints of lemon verbena, the earthy tang of kumquats, and the heady aroma of lavender. The drink's name comes from the address in the Hamptons where the concoction was created.

One 750-milliliter bottle cachaça
16 ounces water
8 ounces Pineapple-Infused Organic Simple
  Syrup (page 147)
Half of an organic pineapple, peeled and cut
  into 1/2-inch cubes
1 quart organic kumquats, halved (do not peel)
10 organic cherries (pitted, if you prefer)
8 sprigs organic lavender
8 organic lemon verbena leaves

In a large pitcher, combine all of the ingredients, cover, and refrigerate overnight. Serve by pouring the punch over ice cubes into rocks glasses.

measurement equivalents

Please note that all conversions are approximate.

LIQUID CONVERSIONS

U.S.	IMPERIAL	METRIC
1 tsp	—	5 ml
1 tbs	1/2 fl oz	15 ml
2 tbs	1 fl oz	30 ml
3 tbs	1 1/2 fl oz	45 ml
1/4 cup	2 fl oz	60 ml
1/3 cup	2 1/2 fl oz	75 ml
1/3 cup + 1 tbs	3 fl oz	90 ml
1/3 cup + 2 tbs	3 1/2 fl oz	100 ml
1/2 cup	4 fl oz	120 ml
2/3 cup	5 fl oz	150 ml
3/4 cup	6 fl oz	180 ml
3/4 cup + 2 tbs	7 fl oz	200 ml
1 cup	8 fl oz	240 ml
1 cup + 2 tbs	9 fl oz	275 ml
1 1/4 cups	10 fl oz	300 ml
1 1/3 cups	11 fl oz	325 ml
1 1/2 cups	12 fl oz	350 ml
1 2/3 cups	13 fl oz	375 ml
1 3/4 cups	14 fl oz	400 ml
1 3/4 cups + 2 tbs	15 fl oz	450 ml
2 cups (1 pint)	16 fl oz	475 ml
2 1/2 cups	20 fl oz	600 ml
3 cups	24 fl oz	720 ml
4 cups (1 quart)	32 fl oz	945 ml

(1,000 ml is 1 liter)

drink credits

FRESH AND ZESTY

- PEPPERED ANGUS: Angus Winchester, cocktail consultant, London
- FLOR DE BAYA: Jeffrey Morgenthaler, Clyde Common, Portland, OR
- SPICY TANGELO PISCO SOUR: Danielle Tatarin, cocktail consultant and garnish producer, Vancouver, British Columbia
- JALISCO FLOWER: Vincenzo Marianella, cocktail consultant, Los Angeles
- PLAZA PASSION: Laura Schweitzer, The Plaza, New York City
- LA NUEVA VIDA: Allen Katz, director of mixology and spirits education, Southern Wine & Spirits, New York City
- COMING IN HOT!: Carlos Yturria, bar manager, Grand Pu Bah, San Francisco
- SPICY PEPINO: Bobby "G" Gleason, mixologist, Beam Global Spirits & Wine, Las Vegas
- POOLSIDE: Edward Allen, director of beverage operations, the Tao Group, Las Vegas
- SAFFRON MARGARITA: Joan Stagnaro, Saffron Restaurant, Princeville, HI

- GINGER-CILANTRO MULE: Charlotte Voisey, brand ambassador, Hendrick's Gin, New York City
- GRILLED PINEAPPLE–KIWI MARGARITA: Shawn Soole, cocktail consultant, Victoria, British Columbia
- GINGERED BLACKBERRY COOLER: Duggan McDonnell, Cantina, San Francisco
- SILKEBORG COCKTAIL: Derek Brown, sommelier, Komi, Washington, DC
- SUN GOLD ZINGER: Carlos Yturria, bar manager, Grand Pu Bah, San Francisco
- À LA PÊCHE: David Wolowidnyk, bar manager, West Restaurant, Vancouver, British Columbia
- CARIBBEAN SOUR: Cody Robertson, owner, Lingba Restaurant & Lounge, San Francisco
- AUTUMN'S CUP: Neyah White, bar manager, Nopa, San Francisco

LUSH AND FRUITY
- EMPEROR NORTON'S MISTRESS: H. Joseph Ehrmann, proprietor, Elixir, San Francisco
- MILK OF MILLENNIA: Duggan McDonnell, Cantina, San Francisco
- NAZCA COCKTAIL: Steve Manktelow, bar manager, Cocoon, London
- PINEAPPLE CAIPIRINHA: John Hogan, cocktail consultant, Las Vegas
- BLACKBERRY MOJITO: Chris Horton, beverage director, JW Marriott Star Pass Hotel and Resort, Tucson, AZ
- W.C.C. FIZZ: Marcos Tello, cocktail consultant, Los Angeles
- DETOX MARGARITA: Trudy Thomas, director of beverages, Camelback Inn, Scottsdale, AZ
- STRAWBERRY-BASIL MARTINI: Michael Anderson, chef instructor, International Culinary School at The Art Institute of Las Vegas
- KIWI ENVY: Ryan Magarian, cocktail consultant, Portland, OR
- CAIPIRINHA CARAMBA: Kim Haasarud, author and cocktail consultant, Marina del Rey, CA
- VOLUPTUOUS: Carlos Yturria, bar manager, Grand Pu Bah, San Francisco
- KI-WHY-NOT: James Dick, food and beverage manager, El Dorado Kitchen, Sonoma, CA
- AMERICAN BEAUTY: Charlotte Voisey, brand ambassador, Hendrick's Gin, New York City
- GOLDEN GATE FOG: H. Joseph Ehrmann, proprietor, Elixir, San Francisco
- BOW THRUSTER: Tony Abou-Gamin, cocktail consultant, Las Vegas
- BLACK AND TAN: Allen Katz, director of mixology and spirits education, Southern Wine & Spirits, New York City

CLEAN AND CLASSIC
- TAHITIAN COFFEE: Cody Robertson, owner, Lingba Restaurant & Lounge, San Francisco
- GRILLED PERSIMMON OLD FASHIONED: Neyah White, bar manager, Nopa, San Francisco
- PEAR SIDECAR: Chris Lee, director of operations, W Seattle Hotel Bar, Seattle, WA
- ORGANIC AGAVE MARGARITA: Nicole Sharpe, general manager, Cantina 1511, Charlotte, NC
- LUNACY: Somer Perez, cocktail consultant, Couture Cocktail Concepts, New York City
- LAVENDER LEMON DROP: Jon Ojinaga, bar manager, Redwood Room at Clift Hotel, San Francisco
- H.W. VERSION 2.0: Marcos Tello, cocktail consultant, Los Angeles
- NOBODY'S DARLING: Joy Richard, director of operations, Tremont 647, Boston
- PURPLE BASIL GIMLET: Charlotte Voisey, brand ambassador, Hendrick's Gin, New York City
- KENTUCKY CHRISTMAS: Jeffrey Morgenthaler, Clyde Common, Portland, OR

- CHURCHILL DOWNS: Trevor Kallies, manager, Granville Room Kitchen & Cocktail Bar, Vancouver, British Columbia
- HEIRLOOM TOMATO G&T: Cody Robertson, owner, Lingba Restaurant & Lounge, San Francisco

FROM THE GARDEN

- CHERRY TOMATO DAIQUIRI: Jeffrey Morgenthaler, Clyde Common, Portland, OR
- COMING UP ROSES: Junior Merino, cocktail consultant and founder, The Liquid Chef, Inc., New York City
- RELIC: Carlos Yturria, bar manager, Grand Pu Bah, San Francisco
- GREEN GARDEN: Brian Van Flandern, Per Se, New York City
- COPPER POT: Camber Lay, bar manager, Epic Roasthouse, San Francisco
- ALIBI: Carlos Yturria, bar manager, Grand Pu Bah, San Francisco
- LADY SAGE: Ryan Magarian, cocktail consultant, Portland, OR
- ELDERFLOWER FIZZ: Trudy Thomas, director of beverages, Camelback Inn, Scottsdale, AZ
- RAINFOREST GINGER-GREEN-TEA-NI: H. Joseph Ehrmann, proprietor, Elixir, San Francisco
- ARBORETUM: Alberta Straub, cocktail consultant, San Francisco
- SPIKED BLUEBERRY-THYME LEMONADE: Charlotte Voisey, brand ambassador, Hendrick's Gin, New York City
- AU PROVENCE: Jackson Cannon, bar manager, Eastern Standard, Boston
- EDEN: Duggan McDonnell, Cantina, San Francisco
- VANDERBILT AVENUE MARTINI: Jonathan Pogash, cocktail consultant, New York City
- BEET-NYK: David Wolowidnyk, bar manager, West Restaurant, Vancouver, British Columbia
- LILY POND: Junior Merino, cocktail consultant and founder, The Liquid Chef, Inc., New York City

- JESSICA RABBIT: Mirjana Kucan, bar chef, The Hilton, Austin, TX
- SNAP-PEA-IRINHA: Adam Seger, beverage director, Nacional 27, Chicago
- SWEET PEA: Danielle Tatarin, cocktail consultant and garnish entrepreneur, Vancouver, British Columbia
- MEDITATION: David Smucker, Morton's the Steakhouse, Kansas City, MO
- BRIDE OF CELERY: Massimo La Rocca, bar manager, St. George Hotel, Rome, Italy
- SECRET GARDEN: Sierra Zimei, Four Seasons Hotel, San Francisco

PUNCH AND PITCHER

- BANK EXCHANGE PUNCH: H. Joseph Ehrmann, proprietor, Elixir, San Francisco
- DARK AND STORMY: Vanessa Sherwood, Some Like it Raw, Chicago
- BERRY GOOD SANGRIA: Kim Haasarud, author and cocktail consultant, Marina del Rey, CA
- WATERMELON COOLER: Shawn Soole, cocktail consultant, Victoria, British Columbia
- AÇAI-LUM SANGRIA: Duggan McDonnell, Cantina, San Francisco
- MELON SANGRIA: Derek Brown, sommelier, Komi, Washington, DC
- FROZEN SANGRIA RITA: Trudy Thomas, director of beverages, Camelback Inn, Scottsdale, AZ
- PASSION FRUIT SANGRIA: Cody Robertson, owner, Lingba Restaurant & Lounge, San Francisco
- PERFECT WHISKEY PUNCH: Joy Richard, director of operations, Tremont 647, Boston
- A.M. PUNCH: Marcos Tello, cocktail consultant, Los Angeles
- ZESTY TOM: Matt Martinez, The Beverly Hills Hotel and Bungalows, Los Angeles
- GREEN AND WHITE SUMMER SANGRIA: Natalie Bovis-Nelsen, instructor, Sustainable Sips eco-friendly cocktail classes, Marina del Rey, CA

- CHERRY SNAPS: Bridget Albert, cocktail consultant, Chicago
- FROZEN BERRY BELLINI and SANGRI-LA: Kim Haasarud, author and cocktail consultant, Marina del Rey, CA
- CHERRY CHILLER: Somer Perez, cocktail consultant, Couture Cocktail Concepts, New York City
- 146 HIGHLAND TERRACE PUNCH: John Hogan, cocktail consultant, Las Vegas

online resources

ORGANIC VODKA
www.Charbay.com
www.ChristianiaVodka.com
www.CropVodka.com
www.GreenMountainDistillers.com
www.HangarOne.com
www.MaisonJomere.com
  (Utkins UK5 Organic Vodka)
www.OrangeV.com
www.OrganicNationVodka.com
www.PeakSpirits.com
www.PrairieVodka.com
www.PurusVodka.com
www.RainVodka.com
www.ReykaVodka.com
www.SquareOneVodka.com
www.TruOrganicSpirits.com
www.Vodka14.com
www.Vodka360.com

ORGANIC GIN
www.BluecoatGin.com
www.MaisonJomere.com
  (Juniper Green Organic Gin)
www.OrganicNationVodka.com
  (Organic Nation Gin)
www.PeakSpirits.com
  (CapRock Organic Dry Gin)

ORGANIC RUM AND CACHAÇA
www.MaisonJomere.com (Papagayo Organic White Rum, Papagayo Organic Fair Trade Golden Rum, Papagayo Organic Spiced Rum)
www.RhumClement.net
www.CucaFrescaSpirit.com

ORGANIC TEQUILA
www.4Copas.com

ORGANIC WINES AND CHAMPAGNES
www.TheOrganicWineCompany.com
www.OrganicVintners.com

LIQUEURS, ORGANIC AND OTHERWISE
www.alpenz.com (allspice liqueur)
www.LoftLiqueurs.com
www.RhumClement.net (Créole Shrubb liqueur)
www.VeeVLife.com (açai liqueur)

MIXERS, SWEETENERS, AND OTHER INGREDIENTS
www.AlteyaOrganics.com (organic rose water)
www.fever-tree.com (organic sodas, tonic water, and club soda)
www.lilyofthedesert.com (organic aloe vera juice)
www.modmixbeverages.com (organic tonic water, sodas, and cocktail mixers)
www.purelyorganic.com (organic orange blossom honey, rose syrup, and vinegars)
www.qtonic.com (organic tonic water)
www.simplyorganicfoods.com (organic spices, including crystallized ginger and Bourbon-Madagascar and Tahitian vanilla beans)
www.wildhibiscus.com (hibiscus syrup)
www.4Copas.com (organic agave nectar)

index

Note: Page numbers in *italics* refer to photographs.